PILOT MEDICAL
HANDBOOK

Human Factors for Successful Flight

Aviation Supplies & Academics, Inc.
Newcastle, Washington

Pilot Medical Handbook: Human Factors for Successful Flight
Contains articles originally published by the Federal Aviation Administration
and the Civil Aviation Medical Institute.

Compiled and published 2009 by Aviation Supplies & Academics, Inc.

Aviation Supplies & Academics, Inc.
7005 132nd Place SE • Newcastle, Washington 98059-3153
Internet: www.asa2fly.com • Email: asa@asa2fly.com
Visit the ASA website often (**www.asa2fly.com**, Products Updates link) to find updates posted
as a result of FAA revisions to regulations or procedures that may affect this book.

Printed in the United States of America
2012   2011   2010   9 8 7 6 5 4 3 2

ASA-MED-HNDBK
ISBN 1-56027-717-3
    978-1-56027-717-0

Contents

Introduction

Human factors, as it relates to flying an aircraft, is the interaction between the pilot, the flying environment, and the aircraft. The area defined by human factors is complex and is where most errors occur. To safely operate an aircraft, you need to develop an awareness of not only the physiological aspect of flying, but also what influences workload and fatigue, decision making, and situational awareness. It is vital that you understand and appreciate how these factors affect your everyday flying.

Your preflight preparations should include evaluating the airworthiness of the:

- **P**ilot: experience, sleep, food and water, drugs and medications, stress, illness.
- **A**ircraft: fuel, weight (does not exceed maximum), density altitude, takeoff and landing requirements, equipment.
- En**V**ironment: weather conditions and forecast for departure and destination airfields and route of flight, runway lengths.
- **E**xternal pressures: schedules, available alternatives, purpose of flight.

These factors are often remembered mnemonically as PAVE, and it is important for you to consider each of them and establish your own personal minimums for flying.

This book will help you determine whether the PAVE factors are favorable for flight. Being a safe pilot means more than remaining current and having a flight review. In order to make a responsible go/no-go decision, you need to do more than check the weather, file a flight plan and perform a preflight inspection. You also must fully assess your physical and mental state and other situational factors when deciding to take a flight. But good decision making doesn't stop there. Once you are airborne, there are a number of situations that could quickly become emergencies if you do not take corrective action.

The FAA has published articles on various physiological topics that are relevant for pilots. You have probably read about several of them in your flight training: hypoxia, visual illusions, and spatial disorientation. By compiling them together in this handbook, it is our hope that you will increase your knowledge and awareness of all factors you should consider prior to, and during flight.

As pilot-in-command, you are ultimately responsible for the decision to fly an aircraft. Use all the information available to you and make the best-informed go/no-go decision.

1 | Aeronautical Decision Making

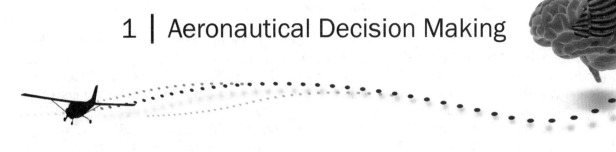

Aeronautical decision making (ADM) is a system-atic approach to the mental process used by airplane pilots to consistently determine the best course of action in response to a given set of circumstances. The importance of learning effective ADM skills cannot be overemphasized. While progress is continually being made in the advancement of pilot training methods, airplane equipment and systems, and services for pilots, accidents still occur. Despite all the changes in technology to improve flight safety, one factor remains the same—the human factor. It is estimated that approximately 75 percent of all aviation accidents are human factors related.

Historically, the term "pilot error" has been used to describe the causes of these accidents. Pilot error means that an action or decision made by the pilot was the cause, or a contributing factor that led to the accident. This definition also includes the pilot's failure to make a decision or take action. From a broader perspective, the phrase "human factors related" more aptly describes these accidents since it is usually not a single decision that leads to an accident, but a chain of events triggered by a number of factors.

The poor judgment chain, sometimes referred to as the "error chain," is a term used to describe this concept of contributing factors in a human factors-related accident. Breaking one link in the chain normally is all that is necessary to change the outcome of the sequence of events. The following is an example illustrating the poor judgment chain.

> **Human Factors**—The study of how people interact with their environments. In the case of general aviation, it is the study of how pilot performance is influenced by such issues as the design of cockpits, the function of the organs of the body, the ef-

fects of emotions, and the interaction and communication with the other participants of the aviation community, such as other crewmembers and air traffic control personnel.

A private pilot with around 350 hours was ferrying an airplane cross-country to a new owner. Due to time constraints, the pilot skipped dinner the night before and had no breakfast on the morning of the flight. The pilot planned to have lunch around noon at a fuel stop.

A descent was begun from 9,500 feet, about 20 miles from the chosen fuel stop, due to haze and unfamiliarity with the area. When the airplane arrived at pattern altitude, the pilot could not find the airport. The pilot then circled north of the town, then back over the town, then flew to the west, then turned back to the east.

The pilot decided to check for airport information in the Airport/Facility Directory, which was on the rear seat and not readily available.

Power had not been increased since the descent to pattern altitude, and the pilot had been holding back pressure on the yoke. While attempting to retrieve the Airport/Facility Directory, a loud "bang" was heard. Looking up, the pilot discovered the airplane was only about 200 feet above ground level. Increasing power, the pilot climbed and located the airport. After landing, it was discovered a fiberglass antenna had been hit, which damaged the leading edge of the left wing.

By discussing the events that led to this accident, it can be understood how a series of judgmental errors contributed to the final outcome of this flight. For example, one of the first elements that affected the pilot's flight was fatigue. The pilot understood that fatigue and hunger could affect the ability to fly safely, but let the desire to stay on schedule override the concern for a safe flight.

Next, the rush to get airborne led the pilot to skip or postpone necessary aspects of preflight planning. Research before takeoff, with a quick review before descent, could have ensured a clear mental picture of the location of the airport in relation to the town. Copying relevant information from flight guides and other information sources is part of careful preflight planning. Studying the aeronautical charts and checking the Notices to Airmen (NOTAM) beforehand would have alerted the pilot to towers, terrain, and other obstructions in the vicinity of the airport.

Even without proper planning before the flight, good cockpit resource management and organization would have had the flight guide and any other necessary information near at hand, perhaps with the relevant pages flagged. Approaching the airport environment and flying around the area at traffic pattern altitude in hazy conditions could have interfered with other air traffic, and the potential for a midair collision is obvious.

In all circumstances, the pilot's first duty is to fly the airplane. Clearly that would include adjusting the power, setting the trim, and keeping track of altitude. This pilot was extremely fortunate—the outcome could easily have been fatal.

On numerous occasions during the flight, the pilot could have made effective decisions that would have broken the chain of errors and prevented this accident. Making sound decisions is the key to preventing accidents. Traditional pilot training has emphasized flying skills, knowledge of the airplane, and familiarity with regulations. ADM training focuses on the decision-making process and the factors that affect a pilot's ability to make effective choices.

Origins of ADM Training

The airlines developed some of the first training programs that focused on improving aeronautical decision-making. Human factor-related accidents motivated the airline industry to implement crew resource management (CRM) training for flight crews. The focus of CRM programs is the effective use of all available resources: human resources, hardware, and information. Human resources include all groups routinely working with the cockpit crew (or pilot) who are involved in decisions that are required to operate a flight safely. These groups include, but are not limited to: dispatchers, cabin crewmembers, maintenance personnel, and air traffic controllers. Although the CRM concept originated as airlines developed ways of facilitating crew cooperation to improve decision making in the cockpit, CRM principles, such as workload management, situational awareness, communication, the leadership role of the captain, and crewmember coordination have direct application to the general aviation cockpit. This also includes single pilot operations since pilots of small airplanes, as well as crews of larger airplanes, must make effective use of all available resources—human resources, hardware, and information. AC 60-22, Aeronautical Decision Making, provides background references, definitions, and other pertinent information about ADM training in the general aviation environment. [Figure 1.1]

The Decision-Making Process

An understanding of the decision-making process provides a pilot with a foundation for developing ADM skills. Some situations, such as engine failures, require a pilot to respond immediately using established procedures with little time for detailed analysis. Traditionally, pilots have been well trained to react to emergencies, but are not as well prepared to make decisions requiring a more reflective response. Typically during a flight, there is time to examine any changes that occur, gather information, and assess risk before reaching a decision. The steps leading to this conclusion constitute the decision-making process.

Defining the Problem

Problem definition is the first step in the decision-making process. Defining the problem begins with recognizing that a change has occurred or that an expected change did not occur. A problem is perceived first by the senses, and then is distinguished through insight and experience. These same abilities, as well as an objective analysis of all available

DEFINITIONS

AERONAUTICAL DECISION MAKING (ADM) is a systematic approach to the mental process used by pilots to consistently determine the best course of action in response to a given set of circumstances.

ATTITUDE is a personal motivational predisposition to respond to persons, situations, or events in a given manner that can, nevertheless, be changed or modified through training as sort of a mental shortcut to decision making.

ATTITUDE MANAGEMENT is the ability to recognize hazardous attitudes in oneself and the willingness to modify them as necessary through the application of an appropriate antidote thought.

HEADWORK is required to accomplish a conscious, rational thought process when making decisions. Good decision making involves risk identification and assessment, information processing, and problem solving.

JUDGMENT is the mental process of recognizing and analyzing all pertinent information in a particular situation, a rational evaluation of alternative actions in response to it, and a timely decision on which action to take.

PERSONALITY is the embodiment of personal traits and characteristics of an individual that are set at a very early age and extremely resistant to change.

POOR JUDGMENT CHAIN is a series of mistakes that may lead to an accident or incident. Two basic principles generally associated with the creation of a poor judgment chain are: (1) One bad decision often leads to another; and (2) as a string of bad decisions grows, it reduces the number of subsequent alternatives for continued safe flight. ADM is intended to break the poor judgment chain before it can cause an accident or incident.

RISK ELEMENTS IN ADM take into consideration the four fundamental risk elements: the pilot, the aircraft, the environment, and the type of operation that comprise any given aviation situation.

RISK MANAGEMENT is the part of the decision-making process which relies on situational awareness, problem recognition, and good judgment to reduce risks associated with each flight.

SITUATIONAL AWARENESS is the accurate perception and understanding of all the factors and conditions within the four fundamental risk elements that affect safety before, during, and after the flight.

SKILLS and PROCEDURES are the procedural, psychomotor, and perceptual skills used to control a specific aircraft or its systems. They are the airmanship abilities that are gained through conventional training, are perfected, and become almost automatic through experience.

STRESS MANAGEMENT is the personal analysis of the kinds of stress experienced while flying, the application of appropriate stress assessment tools, and other coping mechanisms.

CREW RESOURCE MANAGEMENT (CRM) is the application of team management concepts in the flight deck environment. It was initially known as cockpit resource management, but as CRM programs evolved to include cabin crews, maintenance personnel, and others, the phrase crew resource management was adopted. This includes single pilots, as in most general aviation aircraft. Pilots of small aircraft, as well as crews of larger aircraft, must make effective use of all available resources; human resources, hardware, and information. A current definition includes all groups routinely working with the cockpit crew who are involved in decisions required to operate a flight safely.

Figure 1.1 These terms are used in AC 60-22 to explain concepts used in ADM training.

information, are used to determine the exact nature and severity of the problem.

One critical error that can be made during the decision-making process is incorrectly defining the problem. For example, a low oil pressure reading could indicate that the engine is about to fail and an emergency landing should be planned, or it could mean that the oil pressure sensor has failed. The actions to be taken in each of these circumstances would be significantly different. Fixating on a problem that does not exist can divert attention from important tasks. The pilot's failure to maintain an awareness of the circumstances regarding the flight now becomes the problem. This is why once an initial assumption is made regarding the problem, other sources must be used to verify that the conclusion is correct.

While on a cross-country flight, a pilot discovered that fuel consumption was significantly higher than predicted during flight planning. By noticing this discrepancy, change has been recognized. Based on insight, cross-country flying experience, and knowledge of airplane systems, the pilot considers the possibility that there might be enough fuel to reach the destination. Factors that may increase the fuel burn rate could include environmental factors, such as higher-than-expected headwinds and lower-than-expected groundspeed. To determine the severity of the problem, recalculate the fuel consumption and reassess fuel requirements.

Choosing a Course of Action

After the problem has been identified, the pilot must evaluate the need to react to it and determine the actions that may be taken to resolve the situation in the time available. The expected outcome of each possible action should be considered and the risks assessed before deciding on a response to the situation.

The pilot determines there is insufficient fuel to reach the destination, and considers other options, such as turning around and landing at a nearby airport that has been passed, diverting off course, or landing prior to the destination at an airport on the route. The expected outcome of each possible action must be considered along with an assessment of the risks involved. After studying the aeronautical chart, the

pilot concludes that there is an airport that has fueling services within the remaining fuel range along the route. The time expended for the extra fuel stop is a worthwhile investment to ensure a safe completion of the flight.

Implementing the Decision and Evaluating the Outcome

Although a decision may be reached and a course of action implemented, the decision-making process is not complete. It is important to think ahead and determine how the decision could affect other phases of the flight. As the flight progresses, the pilot must continue to evaluate the outcome of the decision to ensure that it is producing the desired result.

To implement the decision, the pilot determines the necessary course changes and calculates a new estimated time of arrival, as well as contacts the nearest flight service station to amend the flight plan and check weather conditions at the fuel stop. Proceeding to the airport, continue to monitor the groundspeed, fuel status, and the weather conditions to ensure that no additional steps need to be taken to guarantee the safety of the flight.

The decision-making process normally consists of several steps before choosing a course of action. To help remember the elements of the decision-making process, a six-step model has been developed using the acronym "DECIDE." [Figure 1.2]

DECIDE MODEL
Detect the fact that a change has occurred.
Estimate the need to counter or react to the change.
Choose a desirable outcome for the success of the flight.
Identify actions which could successfully control the change.
Do the necessary action to adapt to the change.
Evaluate the effect of the action.

Figure 1.2 The DECIDE model can provide a framework for effective decision making.

Risk Elements

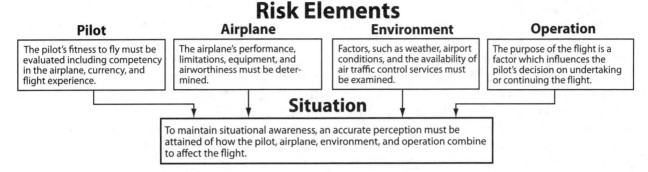

Pilot	Airplane	Environment	Operation
The pilot's fitness to fly must be evaluated including competency in the airplane, currency, and flight experience.	The airplane's performance, limitations, equipment, and airworthiness must be determined.	Factors, such as weather, airport conditions, and the availability of air traffic control services must be examined.	The purpose of the flight is a factor which influences the pilot's decision on undertaking or continuing the flight.

Situation

To maintain situational awareness, an accurate perception must be attained of how the pilot, airplane, environment, and operation combine to affect the flight.

Figure 1.3 When situationally aware, the pilot has an overview of the total operation and is not fixated on one perceived significant factor.

Risk Management

During each flight, decisions must be made regarding events involving interactions between the four risk elements — the pilot in command, the airplane, the environment, and the operation. The decision-making process involves an evaluation of each of these risk elements to achieve an accurate perception of the flight situation. [Figure 1.3]

One of the most important decisions that a pilot in command must make is the go/no-go decision. Evaluating each of these risk elements can help in deciding whether a flight should be conducted or continued. Below is a review of the four risk elements and how they affect decision making regarding the following situations.

Pilot — A pilot must continually make decisions about competency, condition of health, mental and emotional state, level of fatigue, and many other variables. For example, a pilot may be called early in the morning to make a long flight. If a pilot has had only a few hours of sleep and is concerned that the congestion being experienced could be the onset of a cold, it would be prudent to consider if the flight could be accomplished safely.

A pilot had only 4 hours of sleep the night before. The boss then asked the pilot to fly to a meeting in a city 750 miles away. The reported weather was marginal and not expected to improve. After assessing fitness as a pilot, it was decided that it would not be wise to make the flight. The boss was initially unhappy, but later convinced by the pilot that the risks involved were unacceptable.

Airplane — A pilot will frequently base decisions on the evaluations of the airplane, such as performance, equipment, or airworthiness.

During a preflight, a pilot noticed a small amount of oil dripping from the bottom of the cowling. Although the quantity of oil seemed insignificant at the time, the pilot decided to delay the takeoff and have a mechanic check the source of the oil. The pilot's good judgment was confirmed when the mechanic found that one of the oil cooler hose fittings was loose.

Environment — This encompasses many elements not pilot or airplane related. It can include such factors as weather, air traffic control, navaids, terrain, takeoff and landing areas, and surrounding obstacles. Weather is one element that can change drastically over time and distance.

A pilot was landing a small airplane just after a heavy jet had departed a parallel runway. The pilot assumed that wake turbulence would not be a problem since landings had been performed under similar circumstances. Due to a combination of prevailing winds and wake turbulence from the heavy jet drifting across the landing runway, the airplane made a hard landing. The pilot made an error when assessing the flight environment.

Operation — The interaction between the pilot, airplane, and the environment is greatly influenced by the purpose of each flight operation. The pilot must evaluate the three previous areas to decide on the desirability of undertaking or continuing the flight as planned. It is worth asking why the flight is being made, how critical is it to maintain the schedule, and is the trip worth the risks?

On a ferry flight to deliver an airplane from the factory, in marginal weather conditions, the pilot calculated the groundspeed and determined that the airplane would arrive at the destination with only 10 minutes of fuel remaining. The pilot was determined to keep on schedule by trying to "stretch" the fuel supply instead of landing to refuel. After landing with low fuel state, the pilot realized that this could have easily resulted in an emergency landing in deteriorating weather conditions. This was a chance that was not worth taking to keep the planned schedule.

Assessing Risk

Examining National Transportation Safety Board (NTSB) reports and other accident research can help assess risk more effectively. For example, the accident rate during night VFR decreases by nearly 50 percent once a pilot obtains 100 hours, and continues to decrease until the 1,000-hour level. The data suggest that for the first 500 hours, pilots flying VFR at night might want to establish higher personal limitations than are required by the regulations and, if applicable, apply instrument flying skills in this environment. [Figure 1.4]

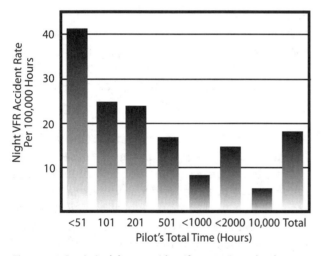

Figure 1.4 Statistical data can identify operations that have more risk involved.

Studies also indicate the types of flight activities that are likely to result in the most serious accidents. The majority of fatal general aviation accidents fall under the categories of takeoff/initial climb, maneuvering flight, approaches, and weather. Delving deeper into accident statistics can provide some important details that can help in understanding the risks involved with specific flying situations. For example, maneuvering flight is one of the largest single producers of fatal accidents. In the approach phase, fatal accidents often happen at night or in IFR conditions. Takeoff/initial climb accidents frequently are due to the pilot's lack of awareness of the effects of density altitude on airplane performance or other improper takeoff planning resulting in loss of control during, or shortly after takeoff. The majority of weather-related accidents occur after attempted VFR flight into IFR conditions.

Factors Affecting Decision Making

It is important to point out the fact that being familiar with the decision-making process does not ensure the good judgment to be a safe pilot. The ability to make effective decisions as pilot in command depends on a number of factors. Some circumstances, such as the time available to make a decision may be beyond a pilot's control. However, one can learn to recognize those factors that can be managed, and learn skills to improve decision-making ability and judgment.

Pilot Self-Assessment

The pilot in command of an airplane is directly responsible for, and is the final authority as to, the operation of that airplane. To effectively exercise that responsibility and make effective decisions regarding the outcome of a flight, a pilot should be aware of personal limitations. Performance during a flight is affected by many factors, such as health, recency of experience, knowledge, skill level, and attitude.

Exercising good judgment begins prior to taking the controls of an airplane. Often, pilots thoroughly check their airplane to determine airworthiness, yet do not evaluate their own fitness for flight. Just as a checklist is used when preflighting an airplane, a personal checklist based on such factors as experience, currency, and comfort level can help determine if a pilot is prepared for a particular flight. Specifying when refresher training should be accomplished and designating weather minimums that may be higher than those listed in Title 14 of the Code of Federal Regulations (14 CFR) part 91 are elements that may be included on a personal checklist. In addition to a review of personal limitations, use the I'M SAFE Checklist to further evaluate fitness for flight. [Figure 1.5]

I'M SAFE CHECKLIST
Illness—Do I have any symptoms?
Medication—Have I been taking prescription or over-the-counter drugs?
Stress—Am I under psychological pressure from the job? Worried about financial matters, health problems, or family discord?
Alcohol—Have I been drinking within 8 hours? Within 24 hours?
Fatigue—Am I tired and not adequately rested?
Eating—Am I adequately nourished?

Figure 1.5 Prior to flight, pilot fitness should be assessed the same as the airplane's airworthiness is evaluated.

THE FIVE HAZARDOUS ATTITUDES
Anti-Authority: "Don't tell me."
This attitude is found in people who do not like anyone telling them what to do. In a sense, they are saying, "No one can tell me what to do." They may be resentful of having someone tell them what to do, or may regard rules, regulations, and procedures as silly or unnecessary. However, it is always your prerogative to question authority if you feel it is in error.
Impulsivity: "Do it quickly."
This is the attitude of people who frequently feel the need to do something, anything, immediately. They do not stop to think about what they are about to do; they do not select the best alternative, but they do the first thing that comes to mind.
Invulnerability: "It won't happen to me."
Many people feel that accidents happen to others, but never to them. They know accidents can happen, and they know that anyone can be affected. They never really feel or believe that they will be personally involved. Pilots who think this way are more likely to take chances and increase risk.
Macho: "I can do it."
Pilots who are always trying to prove that they are better than anyone else are thinking, "I can do it—I'll show them." Pilots with this type of attitude will try to prove themselves by taking risks in order to impress others. While this pattern is thought to be a male characteristic, women are equally susceptible.
Resignation: "What's the use?"
Pilots who think, "What's the use?" do not see themselves as being able to make a great deal of difference in what happens to them. When things go well, the pilot is apt to think that it is good luck. When things go badly, the pilot may feel that someone is out to get me, or attribute it to bad luck. The pilot will leave the action to others, for better or worse. Sometimes, such pilots will even go along with unreasonable requests just to be a "nice guy."

Figure 1.6 The pilot should examine decisions carefully to ensure that the choices have not been influenced by a hazardous attitude.

HAZARDOUS ATTITUDES	ANTIDOTES
Anti-Authority—Although he knows that flying so low to the ground is prohibited by the regulations, he feels that the regulations are too restrictive in some circumstances.	**Follow the rules. They are usually right.**
Impulsivity — As he is buzzing the park, the airplane does not climb as well as Steve had anticipated and without thinking, Steve pulls back hard on the yoke. The airspeed drops and the airplane is close to a stalling attitude as the wing brushes a power line.	**Not so fast. Think first.**
Invulnerability — Steve is not worried about an accident since he has flown this low many times before and he has not had any problems.	**It could happen to me.**
Macho — Steve often brags to his friends about his skills as a pilot and how close to the ground he flies. During a local pleasure flight in his single-engine airplane, he decides to buzz some friends barbecuing at a nearby park.	**Taking chances is foolish.**
Resignation — Although Steve manages to recover, the wing sustains minor damage. Steve thinks to himself, "It's dangerous for the power company to put those lines so close to a park. If somebody finds out about this I'm going to be in trouble, but it seems like no matter what I do, somebody's always going to criticize."	**I'm not helpless. I can make a difference.**

Figure 1.7 *The pilot must be able to identify hazardous attitudes and apply the appropriate antidote when needed.*

Recognizing Hazardous Attitudes

Being fit to fly depends on more than just a pilot's physical condition and recency of experience. For example, attitude will affect the quality of decisions. Attitude can be defined as a personal motivational predisposition to respond to persons, situations, or events in a given manner. Studies have identified five hazardous attitudes that can interfere with the ability to make sound decisions and exercise authority properly. [Figure 1.6]

Hazardous attitudes can lead to poor decision making and actions that involve unnecessary risk. The pilot must examine decisions carefully to ensure that the choices have not been influenced by hazardous attitudes and be familiar with positive alternatives to counteract the hazardous attitudes. These substitute attitudes are referred to as antidotes. During a flight operation, it is important to be able to recognize a hazardous attitude, correctly label the thought, and then recall its antidote. [Figure 1.7]

Stress Management

Everyone is stressed to some degree almost all the time. A certain amount of stress is good since it keeps a person alert and prevents complacency. However, effects of stress are cumulative and, if not coped with adequately, they eventually add up to an intolerable burden. Performance generally increases with the onset of stress, peaks, and then begins to fall off rapidly as stress levels exceed a person's ability to cope.

The ability to make effective decisions during flight can be impaired by stress. Factors, referred to as stressors, can increase a pilot's risk of error in the cockpit. [Figure1.8]

STRESSORS
Physical Stress—Conditions associated with the environment, such as temperature and humidity extremes, noise, vibration, and lack of oxygen.
Physiological Stress—Physical conditions, such as fatigue, lack of physical fitness, sleep loss, missed meals (leading to low blood sugar levels), and illness.
Psychological Stress—Social or emotional factors, such as a death in the family, a divorce, a sick child, or a demotion at work. This type of stress may also be related to mental workload, such as analyzing a problem, navigating an aircraft, or making decisions.

Figure 1.8 *The three types of stressors that can affect a pilot's performance.*

There are several techniques to help manage the accumulation of life stresses and prevent stress overload. For example, including relaxation time in a busy schedule and maintaining a program of physical fitness can help reduce stress levels. Learning to manage time more effectively can help avoid heavy pressures imposed by getting behind schedule and not meeting deadlines. Take a self-assessment to determine capabilities and limitations and then set realistic goals. In addition, avoiding stressful situations and encounters can help to cope with stress.

Use of Resources

To make informed decisions during flight operations, a pilot must become aware of the resources found both inside and outside the cockpit. Since useful tools and sources of information may not always be readily apparent, learning to recognize these resources is an essential part of ADM training. Resources must not only be identified, but a pilot must develop the skills to evaluate whether there is time to use a particular resource and the impact that its use will have upon the safety of flight. For example, the assistance of air traffic control (ATC) may be very useful if a pilot becomes lost. However, in an emergency situation when action needs to be taken quickly, time may not be available to contact ATC immediately.

Internal Resources

Internal resources are found in the cockpit during flight. Since some of the most valuable internal resources are ingenuity, knowledge, and skill, a pilot can expand cockpit resources immensely by improving these capabilities. This can be accomplished by frequently reviewing flight information publications, such as the CFRs and the *Aeronautical Information Manual* (AIM), as well as by pursuing additional training.

A thorough understanding of all the equipment and systems in the airplane is necessary to fully utilize all resources. For example, advanced navigation and autopilot systems are valuable resources. However, if pilots do not fully understand how to use this equipment, or they rely on it so much that they become complacent, it can become a detriment to safe flight.

Checklists are essential cockpit resources for verifying that the airplane instruments and systems are checked, set, and operating properly, as well as ensuring that the proper procedures are performed if there is a system malfunction or in-flight emergency. In addition, the Airplane Flight Manual/Pilot's Operating Handbook (AFM/POH), which is required to be carried on board the airplane, is essential for accurate flight planning and for resolving in-flight equipment malfunctions. Other valuable cockpit resources include current aeronautical charts and publications, such as the Airport/Facility Directory. Passengers can also be a valuable resource. Passengers can help watch for traffic and may be able to provide information in an irregular situation, especially if they are familiar with flying. A strange smell or sound may alert a passenger to a potential problem. A pilot in command should brief passengers before the flight to make sure that they are comfortable voicing any concerns.

External Resources

Possibly the greatest external resources during flight are air traffic controllers and flight service specialists. ATC can help decrease pilot workload by providing traffic advisories, radar vectors, and assistance in emergency situations. Flight service stations can provide updates on weather, answer questions about airport conditions, and may offer direction-finding assistance. The services provided by ATC can be invaluable in enabling a pilot to make informed in-flight decisions.

Workload Management

Effective workload management ensures that essential operations are accomplished by planning, prioritizing, and sequencing tasks to avoid work overload. As experience is gained, a pilot learns to recognize future workload requirements and can prepare for high workload periods during times of low workload. Reviewing the appropriate chart and setting radio frequencies well in advance of when they are needed helps reduce workload as the flight nears the airport. In addition, a pilot should listen to ATIS, ASOS, or AWOS, if available, and then monitor the tower frequency or CTAF to get a good idea of what traffic conditions to expect. Checklists should be performed well in advance so there is time to focus on traffic and ATC instructions. These procedures are especially important prior to entering a high-density traffic area, such as Class B airspace.

To manage workload, items should be prioritized. During any situation, and especially in an emergency, remember the phrase "aviate, navigate, and communicate." This means that the first thing the pilot should do is to make sure the airplane is under control. Then begin flying to an acceptable landing area. Only after the first two items are assured should the pilot try to communicate with anyone.

Another important part of managing workload is recognizing a work overload situation. The first effect of high workload is that the pilot begins to work faster. As workload increases, attention cannot be devoted to several tasks at one time, and the pilot may begin to focus on one item. When a pilot becomes task saturated, there is no awareness of inputs from various sources, so decisions may be made on incomplete information, and the possibility of error increases. [Figure 1.9]

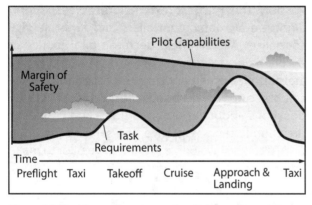

Figure 1.9 Accidents often occur when flying task requirements exceed pilot capabilities. The difference between these two factors is called the margin of safety. Note that in this idealized example, the margin of safety is minimal during the approach and landing. At this point, an emergency or distraction could overtax pilot capabilities, causing an accident.

When becoming overloaded, stop, think, slow down, and prioritize. It is important to understand options that may be available to decrease workload. For example, tasks such as locating an item on a chart or setting a radio frequency may be delegated to another pilot or passenger; an autopilot, if available, may be used; or ATC may be enlisted to provide assistance.

Situational Awareness

Situational awareness is the accurate perception of the operational and environmental factors that affect the airplane, pilot, and passengers during a specific period of time. Maintaining situational awareness requires an understanding of the relative significance of these factors and their future impact on the flight. When situationally aware, the pilot has an overview of the total operation and is not fixated on one perceived significant factor. Some of the elements inside the airplane to be considered are the status of airplane systems, and also the pilot and passengers. In addition, an awareness of the environmental conditions of the flight, such as spatial orientation of the airplane, and its relationship to terrain, traffic, weather, and airspace must be maintained.

To maintain situational awareness, all of the skills involved in aeronautical decision making are used. For example, an accurate perception of pilot fitness can be achieved through self-assessment and recognition of hazardous attitudes. A clear assessment of the status of navigation equipment can be obtained through workload management, and establishing a productive relationship with ATC can be accomplished by effective resource use.

Obstacles to Maintaining Situational Awareness

Fatigue, stress, and work overload can cause a pilot to fixate on a single perceived important item rather than maintaining an overall awareness of the flight situation. A contributing factor in many accidents is a distraction that diverts the pilot's attention from monitoring the instruments or scanning outside the airplane. Many cockpit distractions begin as a minor problem, such as a gauge that is not reading correctly, but result in accidents as the pilot diverts attention to the perceived problem and neglects to properly control the airplane.

Complacency presents another obstacle to maintaining situational awareness. When activities become routine, there is a tendency to relax and not put as much effort into performance. Like fatigue, complacency reduces a pilot's effectiveness in the cockpit. However, complacency is harder to recognize than fatigue, since everything is perceived to be progressing smoothly. For example, a pilot has not bothered to calculate the CG of the airplane because it has never been a problem. Without the pilot realizing it, a passenger loads a heavy piece of equipment in the nose baggage compartment. The pilot notices severe nose heaviness during climbout after takeoff, and finds it necessary to use full nose-up trim to maintain level flight. As the pilot flares for landing, the elevator reaches the stop without raising the nose enough, and the nose-first landing results in loss of the nose gear and extensive damage to the airplane.

Operational Pitfalls

There are a number of classic behavioral traps into which pilots have been known to fall. Pilots, particularly those with considerable experience, as a rule, always try to complete a flight as planned, please passengers, and meet schedules. The basic drive to meet or exceed goals can have an adverse effect on safety, and can impose an unrealistic assessment of piloting skills under stressful conditions. These tendencies ultimately may bring about practices that are dangerous and often illegal, and may lead to a mishap. A pilot will develop awareness and learn to avoid many of these operational pitfalls through effective ADM training. [Figure 1.10]

OPERATIONAL PITFALLS
Peer Pressure — Poor decision making may be based upon an emotional response to peers, rather than evaluating a situation objectively.
Mind Set — A pilot displays mind set through an inability to recognize and cope with changes in a given situation.
Get-There-Itis — This disposition impairs pilot judgment through a fixation on the original goal or destination, combined with a disregard for any alternative course of action.
Duck-Under Syndrome — A pilot may be tempted to make it into an airport by descending below minimums during an approach. There may be a belief that there is a built-in margin of error in every approach procedure, or a pilot may want to admit that the landing cannot be completed and a missed approach must be initiated.
Scud Running — This occurs when a pilot tries to maintain visual contact with the terrain at low altitudes while instrument conditions exist.
Continuing Visual Flight Rules (VFR) into Instrument Conditions — Spatial disorientation or collision with ground/obstacles may occur when a pilot continues VFR into instrument conditions. This can be even more dangerous if the pilot is not instrument rated or current.
Getting Behind the Aircraft — This pitfall can be caused by allowing events or the situation to control pilot actions. A constant state of surprise at what happens next may be exhibited when the pilot is getting behind the aircraft.
Loss of Positional or Situational Awareness — In extreme cases, when a pilot gets behind the aircraft, a loss of positional or situational awareness may result. The pilot may not know the aircraft's geographical location, or may be unable to recognize deteriorating circumstances.
Operating Without Adequate Fuel Reserves — Ignoring minimum fuel reserve requirements is generally the result of overconfidence, lack of flight planning, or disregarding applicable regulations.
Descent Below the Minimum En Route Altitude — The duck-under syndrome, as mentioned above, can also occur during the en route portion of an IFR flight.
Flying Outside the Envelope — The assumed high performance capability of a particular aircraft may cause a mistaken belief that it can meet the demands imposed by a pilot's overestimated flying skills.
Neglect of Flight Planning, Preflight Inspections, and Checklists — A pilot may rely on short- and long-term memory, regular flying skills, and familiar routes instead of established procedures and published checklists. This can be particularly true of experienced pilots.

Figure 1.10 All experienced pilots have fallen prey to, or have been tempted by, one or more of these tendencies in their flying career.

2 | Establishing Personal Minimums

You don't have to be involved in aviation very long before you hear the time-honored advice on personal minimums. It goes something like this: "Legal weather minimums are just a starting point. You should establish your own personal minimums for flying, and you must have the discipline to stick to them—no matter how much you want to make the trip."

Sound familiar? It's good advice. Most pilots would agree that it's a good idea, and it's probably true that more accident pilots—not to mention their innocent passengers—might be alive today if they had followed it. So why didn't they? And why do so many pilots who appear for flight reviews or other training look sheepish and make excuses for why they haven't managed to write down their own personal minimums?

There are probably many reasons that the concept of personal minimums is more honored as an idea than as a regular practice. I suspect, however, that a major reason is that many pilots—even safety-conscious ones—don't have a clear idea about where to start, and that many flight instructors—even conscientious ones—may not know how to guide pilots through the process of establishing personal minimums. I confess that I have been guilty on both counts. I consider myself to be a safety-minded pilot, but for too many years my personal minimums were little more than a vague mental notion. I also like to think of myself as a conscientious and safety-minded flight instructor (CFI), but far too few of my clients would be able to tell you that I even talked about, much less taught about, personal minimums. To make amends, here are some ideas that might help fellow aviators avoid similar sins of omission.

Let's start with the basics. What exactly do we mean when we talk about "personal minimums?" In formal terms, personal minimums refers to an individual pilot's set of procedures, rules, criteria, and guidelines for deciding whether, and under what conditions, to operate (or continue operating) in the National Airspace System. While this definition is accurate, there are several reasons why you may not find it particularly helpful as a starting point. First, it tends to describe the product rather than explain the process, which is where many pilots have trouble. Second, and more importantly, the formal definition of the end product—your personal set of procedures, rules, criteria, and guidelines—does not really convey one of the core concepts: personal minimums as a "safety buffer" between the demands of the situation and the extent of your skills.

Think of personal minimums as the human factors equivalent of reserve fuel. When you plan a flight, the regulations require you to calculate fuel use in a way that leaves a certain minimum amount of fuel in the tanks when you land at your destination or your alternative. The reserve fuel is intended to provide a safety buffer between fuel required for normal flight and fuel available to avoid total quiet in your engine compartment.

In the same way, personal minimums should be set so as to provide a solid safety buffer between the skills required for the specific flight you want to make, and the skills available to you through training, experience, currency, and proficiency. In fuel calculations, you wouldn't dream of planning a flight that would force you to use your reserve fuel, or (worse) take you to the "unusable fuel" level in the tanks. In skill calculations, you shouldn't consider making a flight that requires use of skills at the "reserve" or (worse) "unusable fuel" level of your piloting ability.

So where do you start in developing personal minimums? There is no single "right" way to proceed, but if you're unsure of how to proceed in establishing your own personal minimums, this method offers a reasonable place to start.

Step 1 – Review Weather Minimums

Most people think of personal minimums primarily in terms of weather conditions, so begin with a quick review of weather definitions. The regulations define weather flight conditions for visual flight rules (VFR) and instrument flight rules (IFR) in terms of specific values for ceiling and visibility. [Figure 2.1]

For our purpose, we will define IFR as a ceiling less than 1,000 feet AGL and/or visibility less than three miles. LIFR is a sub-category of IFR. VFR is defined as ceiling greater than 3,000 feet AGL and visibility greater than five miles. MVFR is a sub-category of VFR.

Step 2 – Assess Your Experience and Comfort Level

At first glance, this part of the process might look a bit complicated, but please bear with me. It might take a few minutes to review, record, and summarize your personal experience, but I think you will find that the finished product is well worth your time.

First, think back through your flight training and complete the "Certification, Training, and Experience Summary" chart on the next page. The Certification, Training, and Experience Summary Source is adapted from the FAA's Personal and Weather Risk

Assessment Guide (October 2003). This guide can be found at: www.faa.gov/.

Next, think through your recent flying experiences and make a note of the lowest weather conditions that you have comfortably experienced as a pilot in your VFR and, if applicable, IFR flying in the last six to 12 months. You might want to use Figures 2.2, 2.4 and 2.5 as a guide for this assessment, but don't feel that you need to fill in every square. In fact, you may not have, or even need, an entry for every category. For example, suppose that most of your flying takes place in a part of the country where clear skies and visibilities of 30 plus miles are normal. Your entry might specify the lowest VFR ceiling as 7,000, and the lowest visibility as 15 miles. You may have never experienced MVFR conditions at all, so you would leave those boxes blank.

In my part of the country, normal summer flying often involves hazy conditions, but over relatively flat terrain. I know the local terrain and, since I have regularly operated in hazy daytime MVFR conditions (e.g., 2,500 and four miles), I would use the MVFR column to record these values. Even in my home airspace, though, I would not consider flying down to VFR minimums at night — much less in the range of conditions defined as MVFR. For night VFR, I would not be comfortable with anything less than a ceiling of at least 5,000, and visibility of at least seven to eight miles. How my entries would look in the Experience & "Comfort Level" Assessment VFR & MFR chart. [Figure 2.2]

If you fly IFR, the next part of the exercise is to record the lowest IFR conditions that you have comfortably, recently and regularly experienced in your flying career. Again, be honest in your assessment.

CATEGORY	CEILING		VISIBILITY
Visual Flight Rules VFR (green sky symbol)	greater than 3,000 feet AGL	and	greater than 5 miles
Marginal Visual Flight Rules MVFR (blue sky symbol)	1,000 to 3,000 feet AGL	and/or	3 to 5 miles
Instrument Flight Rules IFR (red sky symbol)	500 to below 1,000 feet AGL	and/or	1 mile to less than 3 miles
Low Instrument Flight Rules LIFR (magenta sky symbol)	below 500 feet AGL	and/or	less than 1 mile

Figure 2.1 Weather minimums.

Experience & "Comfort Level" Assessment VFR & MVFR		
Weather Condition	**VFR**	**MVFR**
Ceiling	> 3,000	1,000-3,000
Day	—	2,500
Night	5,000	—
Visibility	> 5 miles	3-5 miles
Day	—	4 miles
Night	8 miles	—

Figure 2.2 Experience and Comfort Level Assessment VFR & MVFR.

CERTIFICATION LEVEL	
Certification level (e.g., private, commercial, ATP)	
Ratings (e.g., Instrument, multi-engine)	
Endorsements (e.g., complex, high performance, high altitude)	
TRAINING SUMMARY	
Flight review (e.g., certificate, rating, Wings)	
Instrument Proficiency Check	
Time since checkout in airplane 1	
Time since checkout in airplane 2	
Time since checkout in airplane 3	
Variation in equipment (e.g., GPS navigators, autopilot)	
EXPERIENCE	
Total flying time	
Years of flying experience	
RECENT EXPERIENCE (last 12 months)	
Hours	
Hours in this airplane (or identical model)	
Landings	
Night hours	
Night landings	
Hours flown in high density altitude	
Hours flown in mountainous terrain	
Crosswind landings	
IFR hours	
IMC hours (actual conditions)	
Approaches (actual or simulated)	

Figure 2.3 Certification, training, and experience summary.

Although I have successfully flown in low IFR (LIFR) conditions — down to a 300 foot ceiling and 3/4 mile visibility — I would never claim to have been "comfortable" in these conditions, especially since I was operating in a single pilot/single engine configuration. I would therefore leave the LIFR boxes blank, and my entries for known "comfort level" in Instrument Meteorological Conditions (IMC) would be as shown in Figure 2.4.

Experience & "Comfort Level" Assessment IFR & LIFR		
Weather Condition	IFR	LIFR
Ceiling	500-999	< 500
Day	800	—
Night	999	—
Visibility	1-3 miles	< 1 mile
Day	1 mile	—
Night	3 miles	—

Figure 2.4 Experience & "Comfort Level" Assessment IFR & LIFR.

If I combine my entries into a single chart, the summary of my personal known "comfort level" for VFR, MVFR, IFR, and LIFR weather conditions is as follows:

Experience & "Comfort Level" Assessment VFR & IFR		
Weather Condition	VFR/ MVFR	IFR/ LIFR
Ceiling		
Day	2,500	800
Night	5,000	999
Visibility		
Day	4 miles	1 mile
Night	8 miles	3 miles

Figure 2.5 Experience & "Comfort Level" Assessment VFR & IFR.

Step 3 – Consider Other Conditions

Ceiling and visibility are the most obvious conditions to consider in setting personal minimums, but it is also a good idea to have personal minimums for wind and turbulence. As with ceiling and

visibility, the goal in this step is to record the most challenging wind conditions you have comfortably experienced in the last six to 12 months — not necessarily the most challenging wind conditions you have managed to survive without bending an airplane. As shown in Figure 2.6, you can record these values for category and class, for specific make and model, or perhaps both.

Experience & "Comfort Level" Assessment Wind & Turbulence			
Turbulence	SE	ME	Make/ Model
Surface wind speed	10 knots	15 knots	
Surface wind gusts	5 knots	8 knots	
Crosswind component	7	7	

Figure 2.6 Experience & "Comfort Level" Assessment Wind & Turbulence.

In addition to winds, your "comfort level" inventory should also include factors related to aircraft performance. There are many variables, but start by completing the chart with reference to the aircraft and terrain most typical for the kind of flying you do most. Remember that you want to establish a safety buffer, so be honest with yourself. If you have never operated to/from a runway shorter than 5,000 feet, the "shortest runway" box should say 5,000 feet. [Figure 2.7] We will talk more about safe ways to extend personal minimums a bit later.

Experience & "Comfort Level" Assessment Performance Factors			
Performance	SE	ME	Make/ Model
Shortest runway	2,500	4,500	
Highest terrain	6,000	3,000	
Highest density altitude	3,000	3,000	

Figure 2.7 Experience & "Comfort Level" Assessment Performance Factors.

Step 4 – Assemble and Evaluate

Now you have some useful numbers to use in establishing baseline personal minimums. Combining these numbers the Baseline Personal Minimums chart, Figure 2.8 shows how the whole picture might look.

Step 5 – Adjust for Specific Conditions

Any flight you make involves almost infinite combinations of pilot skill, experience, condition, and proficiency; aircraft equipment and performance; environmental conditions; and external influences. Both individually and in combination, these factors can compress the safety buffer provided by your baseline personal minimums. Consequently, you need a practical way to adjust your baseline personal minimums to accommodate specific conditions. See Figure 2.9 for an example of how this can be done.

Note that the suggested adjustment factors are just that — a suggestion. If your flying experience is limited or if you don't fly very often, you might want to double these values. In addition, if your situation involves more than one special condition from Figure 2.9, you will probably want to add the adjustment factor for each one. For example, suppose you are planning a night cross-country to an unfamiliar airport, departing after a full workday. If you decide to make this trip — or you might decide that it is safest to wait until the next day — this chart suggests that you should at least raise your baseline personal minimums by adding 1,000 feet to your ceiling value; one mile to visibility, and 1,000 feet to required runway length.

How about adjustments in the other direction? Some pilots fear that establishing personal minimums is a once-and-for-all exercise. With time and experience, though, you can modify personal minimums to match growing skill and judgment. When you have comfortably flown to your baseline personal minimums for several months, you might want to sit down and assess whether, and how, to safely push the envelope. If, for instance, your personal minimums call for daytime visibility of at least five miles, and you have developed some solid experience flying in those conditions, you might consider lowering the visibility value to four miles for your next flight.

Experience & "Comfort Level" Assessment Performance Factors				
Weather Conditions	**VFR**	**MVFR**	**IFR**	**LIFR**
Ceiling				
Day	2,500		800	
Night	5,000		999	
Visibility				
Day	4 miles		1 mile	
Night	8 miles		3 miles	
Turbulence	**SE**	**ME**	**Make/Model**	
Surface wind speed	10 knots	15 knots		
Surface wind gusts	5 knots	8 knots		
Crosswind component	7	7		
Performance	**SE**	**ME**	**Make/Model**	
Shortest runway	2,500	4,500		
Highest terrain	6,000	3,000		
Highest density altitude	3,000	3,000		

Figure 2.8 Experience & "Comfort Level" Assessment Performance Factors.

Two important cautions:

- First, never adjust personal minimums to a lower value for a specific flight. The time to consider adjustments is when you are not under any pressure to fly, and when you have the time and objectivity to think honestly about your skill, performance, and comfort level during last the few flights. Changing personal minimums for visibility, don't try to lower the ceiling, wind, or other values at the same time. In addition, you never want to push the baseline if there are special conditions (e.g., unfamiliar aircraft, pilot fatigue) present for this flight.

- Second, keep all other variables constant. For example, if your goal is to lower your baseline personal minimums for visibility, don't try to lower the ceiling, wind, or other values at the same time. In addition, you never want to push the baseline if there are special conditions (e.g., unfamiliar aircraft, pilot fatigue) present for this flight.

You might find it helpful to talk through both your newly established personal minimums and any "push-the-envelope" plans with a well-qualified flight instructor.

Step 6 – Stick to the Plan!

Once you have done all the thinking required to establish baseline personal minimums, "all" you need to do next is stick to the plan. As most pilots know, that task is a lot harder than it sounds, especially when the flight is for a trip that you really want to make, or when you are staring into the faces of your disappointed passengers. Here's where personal minimums can be an especially valuable tool. Professional pilots live by the numbers, and so should you. Pre-established hard numbers can make it a lot easier to make a smart "no go" or "divert" decision than a vague sense that you can "probably" deal with the conditions that you are facing at any given time. In addition, a written set of personal minimums can also make it easier to explain tough decisions to passengers who are, after all, trusting their lives to your aeronautical skill and judgment.

Susan Parson is a Special Assistant in Flight Standards' General Aviation and Commercial Division and an active general aviation pilot and flight instructor. She welcomes your thoughts and ideas on best practices for establishing and adjusting your personal minimums. Send comments to: susan.parson@faa.gov.

	If you are facing:		Adjust baseline personal minimums by:
Pilot	Illness, use of medication, stress, or fatigue; lack of currency (e.g., haven't flown for several weeks)	Add (+)	at least 500 feet to ceiling
			at least 1/2 mile visibility
Aircraft	An unfamiliar airplane or an aircraft with unfamiliar avionics or other equipment		at least 500 ft to runway length
Environment	Unfamiliar airports and airspace; different terrain or other unfamiliar characteristics		
External Pressures	"Must meet" deadlines, pressures from passengers, etc.	Subtract (-)	at least 5 knots from winds

Figure 2.9 Adjust baseline minimums for specific conditions.

3 | Medications and Flying

Does this story sound familiar?

It's Sunday morning, the last day of a three-day trip. You have four hours of flying ahead of you to get back home, but something about the air conditioner last night has left you with stuffy nose and sinuses this morning. You know from your training and experience that flying with congested upper airways is not a good thing. As it turns out, one of the others on the trip has some new over-the-counter sinus pills that are "guaranteed" to unstop your breathing passages and let you fly without any worries about the congestion. *Should you take the medication?*

Another Scenario

You and your spouse are on the second leg of a five-leg, cross-country flight. While visiting relatives, you stayed up late at the party they threw in your honor, ate too much, and the next morning your stomach feels sort of queasy. Your spouse, a non-pilot, offers you a common motion-sickness pill prescribed by her doctor. Should you take the medication?

Get the Facts

Just like any other decision (equipment, weather, etc.) that you must make when you fly, you should know all the facts before you can answer this question. There are several things that you need to know and take into account before you make the go/no-go decision. Add these to your checklist:

First, **consider the underlying condition that you are treating.** What will be the consequences if the medication doesn't work or if it wears off before the flight is over? A good general rule to follow is not to fly if you must depend on the medication to keep the flight safe. In other words, if the untreated condition is one that would prevent safe flying, then you shouldn't fly until the condition improves — whether you take the medication or not.

Second, you must **consider your reaction to the medication.** There are two broad categories of medication reactions. One is a unique reaction based on an individual's biological make-up. Most people don't have such reactions but anyone can, given the right medication. Because of this, you should NEVER fly after taking any medication that you have not taken before. It is not until after you have taken the medication that you will find out whether you have this uncommon and unexpected reaction to the medication.

Third, consider the potential for adverse reactions, or side effect — unwanted reactions to medications. This type of reaction is quite common, and the manufacturer of the medication lists these on the label. You MUST carefully read all labeling. If you don't have access to the label, then don't fly while using the medication.

Look for such key words such as lightheadedness, dizziness, drowsiness, or visual disturbance. If these side effects are listed on the label, or if the label contains a warning about operating motor vehicles or machinery, then you should not fly while using the medication.

Side effects can occur at any time, so even if you've taken the same medication in the past without experiencing side effects, they could still occur the next time. For this reason, you must never fly after taking a medication with any of the above-noted side effects. [Figure 3.1]

Common Side Effects of Frequently Used Medications

If you must take over-the-counter medications,

- Read and follow the label directions.
- If the label warns of significant side effects, do not fly after taking the medication until at least two dosing intervals have passed. For example, if the directions say to take the medication every 6 hours, wait until at least 12 hours after the last dose to fly.
- Remember that you should not fly if the underlying condition that you are treating would make you unsafe if the medication fails to work.
- Never fly after taking a new medication for the first time.
- As with alcohol, medications may impair your ability to fly—even though you feel fine.
- If you have questions about a medication, ask your aviation medical examiner.
- When in doubt, don't fly.

Prescription Medications

When your treating physician prescribes a medication for you, be sure to ask about possible side effects and the safety of using the medication while flying. Since most of their patients are not pilots, many physicians don't think about the special needs of pilots when they prescribe medication. You must also discuss the medical condition that is being treated. You may want to ask your physician to contact your aviation medical examiner to discuss the implications of flying with the medical condition and the medication.

When your pharmacy fills the prescription, let the pharmacist know that you are a pilot. Pharmacists are experts in medication side effects and can often provide advice that supplements the information that your physician gives you. The pharmacist will provide you with written information about your medication. You should treat this just like the label of an over-the-counter medication mentioned above. Read, understand, and follow the information and instructions that are given with the medication. Never hesitate to discuss possible problems with your physician, pharmacist, or aviation medical examiner.

Problem	Type of Medication	Example	Potential side effects
Colds, congestion, and allergies	• Decongestant • Antihistamine	Pseudoephedrine (Sudafed®) Diphenhydramine (Benadryl®)	Palpitations, jitteriness, anxiety, drowsiness
Cough	Cough suppressant	Dextromethorphan (Robitussin DM®)	Dizziness, drowsiness
Fever	Antipyretic	Aspirin	Ringing in ears, upset stomach
Pain	Analgesic	Ibuprofen (Motrin®)	Dizziness, upset stomach
Nausea/Vomiting	Antinauseant	Dimenhydranate (Dramamine®)	Drowsiness
Diarrhea	Antidiarrheal	Loperamide (Imodium®)	Drowsiness
Acid reflux	Antacid	Ranitidine (Zantac®)	Headache, nausea
Constipation	Laxative	Various	Abdominal cramping, diarrhea
Overweight	Diet pill	Ephedrine (Ephedra)	Palpitations, jitteriness, anxiety, heart attack, stroke
Insomnia	Sleeping pills	Diphenhydramine (Tylenol PM®)	Prolonged drowsiness and impairment of reaction times

Figure 3.1 Common side effects of frequently used medications.

The Bottom Line

What you must remember about medications:

Sometimes…

…you will develop a medical condition that is not safe to fly with. Whether you take a medication for the condition or not, you should wait to fly until the condition is either gone or significantly improved.

…you will have an ongoing (chronic) medical condition that your physician has prescribed a medication to treat. You should discuss the medical condition and treatment with your physician, pharmacist, and aviation medical examiner and make your flying decision based on their advice.

…you will have a medical condition that makes you uncomfortable but does not impair your ability to safely fly. If flying is very important, you may take either over-the-counter medications or prescription medications — within the guidelines suggested above.

Flying is important for many reasons. Not one of these reasons, however, is worth risking your life or the lives of those around you. Treat all medications with caution, and you'll be around to become one of the "old" pilots.

4 | Alcohol and Flying: Deadly Combination

Alcoholic beverages, used by many to "unwind" or relax, act as a social "ice-breaker," and alter one's mood by decreasing inhibitions. Alcohol consumption is widely accepted, often providing the cornerstone of social gatherings and celebrations. Along with cigarettes, many adolescents associate the use of alcohol as a rite of passage into adulthood.

While its use is prevalent and acceptable in our society, it should not come as a surprise that problems arise in the use of alcohol and the performance of safety-related activities, such as driving an automobile or flying an aircraft. These problems are made worse by the common belief that accidents happen "to other people, but not to me." There is a tendency to forget that flying an aircraft is a highly demanding cognitive and psychomotor task that takes place in an inhospitable environment where pilots are exposed to various sources of stress.

Hard Facts About Alcohol

- It's a sedative, hypnotic, and addicting drug.
- Alcohol quickly impairs judgment and leads to behavior that can easily contribute to, or cause accidents.

The Erratic Effects of Alcohol

- Alcohol is rapidly absorbed from the stomach and small intestine, and transported by the blood throughout the body. Its toxic effects vary considerably from person to person, and are influenced by variables such as gender, body weight, rate of consumption (time), and total amount consumed.
- The average, healthy person eliminates pure alcohol at a fairly constant rate — about 1/3 to 1/2 oz. of pure alcohol per hour, which is equiv-

alent to the amount of pure alcohol contained in any of the popular drinks listed in Figure 4.1. This rate of elimination of alcohol is relatively constant, regardless of the total amount of alcohol consumed. In other words, whether a person consumes a few or many drinks, the rate of alcohol elimination from the body is essentially the same. Therefore, the more alcohol an individual consumes, the longer it takes his/her body to get rid of it.

- Even after complete elimination of all of the alcohol in the body, there are undesirable effect — hangover — that can last 48 to 72 hours following the last drink.
- The majority of adverse effects produced by alcohol relate to the brain, the eyes, and the inner ear — three crucial organs to a pilot.
- Brain effects include impaired reaction time, reasoning, judgment, and memory. Alcohol decreases the ability of the brain to make use of oxygen. This adverse effect can be magnified as a result of simultaneous exposure to altitude, characterized by a decreased partial pressure of oxygen.
- Visual symptoms include eye muscle imbalance, which leads to double vision and difficulty focusing.
- Inner ear effects include dizziness and decreased hearing perception.
- If other variables are added, such as sleep deprivation, fatigue, medication use, altitude hypoxia, or flying at night or in bad weather, the negative effects are significantly magnified.

Type of Beverage	Typical Serving (oz.)	Pure Alcohol Content (oz.)
Table wine	4	.48
Light Beer	12	.48
Aperitif Liquor	1.5	.38
Champagne	4	.48
Vodka	1	.50
Whiskey	1.25	.50

Figure 4.1 Amount of alcohol in various alcoholic beverages.

Figure 4.2 summarizes some of the effects of various blood alcohol concentrations. The blood alcohol content values in the table overlap because of the wide variation in alcohol tolerance among individuals.

Studies of How Alcohol Affects Pilot Performance

- Pilots have shown impairment in their ability to fly an ILS approach or to fly IFR, and even to perform routine VFR flight tasks while under the influence of alcohol, regardless of individual flying experience.

- The number of serious errors committed by pilots dramatically increases at or above concentrations of 0.04% blood alcohol. This is not to say that problems don't occur below this value. Some studies have shown decrements in pilot performance with blood alcohol concentrations as low as the 0.025%.

Studies of Fatal Accidents

Figure 4.3 shows the annual alcohol-related pilot fatalities in general aviation accidents between 1987 and 1993, as reported by the Forensic Toxicology Research Section of the FAA Civil Aerospace Medical Institute. This information is based on the analysis of blood and tissue samples from pilots involved in fatal aviation accidents.

Hangovers are Dangerous

A hangover effect, produced by alcoholic beverages after the acute intoxication has worn off, may be just as dangerous as the intoxication itself. Symptoms commonly associated with a hangover are headache, dizziness, dry mouth, stuffy nose, fatigue, upset stomach, irritability, impaired judgment, and increased sensitivity to bright light. A pilot with these symptoms would certainly not be fit to safely operate an aircraft. In addition, such a pilot could readily be perceived as being "under the influence of alcohol."

You are in Control

Flying, while fun and exciting, is a precise, demanding, and unforgiving endeavor. Any factor that impairs the pilot's ability to perform the required tasks during the operation of an aircraft is an invitation for disaster.

0.01-0.05 (10-50 mg%)	average individual appears normal
0.03-0.12* (30-120 mg%)	mild euphoria, talkativeness, decreased inhibitions, decreased attention, impaired judgment, increased reaction time
0.09-0.25 (90-250 mg%)	emotional instability, loss of critical judgment, impairment of memory and comprehension, decreased sensory response, mild muscular incoordination
0.18-0.30 (180-300 mg%)	confusion, dizziness, exaggerated emotions (anger, fear, grief), impaired visual perception, decreased pain sensation, impaired balance, staggering gait, slurred speech, moderate muscular incoordination
0.27-0.40 (270-400 mg%)	apathy, impaired consciousness, stupor, significantly decreased response to stimulation, severe muscular incoordination, inability to stand or walk, vomiting, incontinence of urine and feces
0.35-0.50 350-500 mg%	unconsciousness, depressed or abolished reflexes, abnormal body temperature, coma, possible death from respiratory paralysis (450 mg% or above)

* Legal limit for motor vehicle operation in most states is .08 or .10% (80-100 mg of alcohol per dL of blood).

Figure 4.2 Some of the effects of various blood alcohol concentrations.

Year	General Aviation Pilot Facilities	Pilots with BAC of 0.02% or more*	Pilots with BAC of 0.04% or more*
1987	341	13.5%	8.5%
1988	364	6.6%	6.3%
1989	349	12.9%	8.0%
1990	367	14.2%	7.9%
1991	379	12.9%	7.9%
1992	396	11.9%	7.3%
1993	338	12.7%	8.9%

*Some cases may include alcohol produced after death by tissue decomposition. BAC = Blood alcohol concentration

Figure 4.3 Fatal general aviation accidents with alcohol as possible contributing factor.

The use of alcohol is a significant self-imposed stress factor that should be eliminated from the cockpit. The ability to do so is strictly within the pilot's control.

Keep in mind that regulations alone are no guarantee that problems won't occur. It is far more important for pilots to understand the negative effects of alcohol and its deadly impact on flight safety.

General Recommendations

1. As a minimum, adhere to all the guidelines of FAR 91.17: [Figure 4.4]
   • 8 hours from "bottle to throttle"
   • Do not fly while under the influence of alcohol
   • Do not fly while using any drug that may adversely affect safety
2. A more conservative approach is to wait 24 hours from the last use of alcohol before flying. This is especially true if intoxication occurred or if you plan to fly IFR. Cold showers, drinking black coffee, or breathing 100% oxygen cannot speed up the elimination of alcohol from the body.
3. Consider the effects of a hangover. Eight hours from "bottle to throttle" does not mean you are in the best physical condition to fly, or that your blood alcohol concentration is below the legal limits.

4. Recognize the hazards of combining alcohol consumption and flying.
5. Use good judgment. Your life and the lives of your passengers are at risk if you drink and fly.

Ideally, total avoidance of alcohol should be a key element observed by every pilot in planning or accomplishing a flight.

Alcohol avoidance is as critical as developing a flight plan, a good preflight inspection, obeying ATC procedures, and avoiding severe weather.

Federal Aviation Regulation (FAR) 91.17

The use of alcohol and drugs by pilots is regulated by FAR 91.17. Among other provisions, this regulation states that no person may operate or attempt to operate an aircraft:

• within 8 hours of having consumed alcohol
• while under the influence of alcohol
• with a blood alcohol content of 0.04% or greater
• while using any drug that adversely affects safety

Figure 4.4 Federal Aviation Regulation Part 91.17.

Alcohol Use In America

• Over 50% of American adults consume alcohol.
• Per capita consumption is about 25 gallons per year.
• Alcoholic beverages are marketed in a variety of forms, with wine and beer being the most liked.
• Different alcoholic beverages have different concentrations of alcohol; however, their total alcohol content can be the same. For example, a pint of beer contains as much alcohol as a 5-1/2 ounce glass of table wine. Therefore, the notion that drinking low-concentration alcoholic beverages is safer than drinking hard liquor is erroneous.
• The total alcohol content of any alcoholic beverage can be easily calculated using the following formula: "Proof" divided by 2 = percent pure alcohol.

5 | Fatigue in Aviation

Fatigue is an expected and ubiquitous aspect of life. For the average individual, fatigue presents a minor inconvenience, resolved with a nap or by stopping whatever activity that brought it on. Typically, there are no significant consequences. However, if that person is involved in safety-related activities such as operating a motor vehicle, piloting an aircraft, performing surgery, or running a nuclear reactor, the consequences of fatigue can be disastrous.

Definition

Defining fatigue in humans is extremely difficult due to the large variability of causes. Causes of fatigue can range from boredom to circadian rhythm disruption to heavy physical exertion. In lay terms, fatigue can simply be defined as weariness. However, from an operational standpoint a more accurate definition might be: "Fatigue is a condition characterized by increased discomfort with lessened capacity for work, reduced efficiency of accomplishment, loss of power or capacity to respond to stimulation, and is usually accompanied by a feeling of weariness and tiredness."

Two key concepts can be derived from this second definition:

1. Fatigue can develop from a variety of sources. The important factor is not what causes the fatigue but rather the negative impact fatigue has on a person's ability to perform tasks. A long day of mental stimulation such as studying for an examination or processing data for a report can be as fatiguing as manual labor. They may feel different—a sore body instead of a headache and bleary eyes—but the end effect is the same, an inability to function normally.

2. Fatigue leads to a decrease in your ability to carry out tasks. Several studies have demonstrated significant impairment in a person's ability to carry out tasks that require manual dexterity, concentration, and higher-order intellectual processing. Fatigue may happen acutely, which is to say in a relatively short time (hours) after some significant physical or mental activity. Or, it may occur gradually over several days or weeks. Typically, this situation occurs with someone who does not get sufficient sleep over a prolonged period of time (as with sleep apnea, jet lag, or shift work) or someone who is involved in ongoing physical or mental activity with insufficient rest.

Stressors

General aviation pilots are typically not exposed to the same occupational stresses as commercial pilots (i.e., long duty days, circadian disruptions from night flying or time zone changes, or scheduling changes). Nevertheless, they will still develop fatigue from a variety of other causes. Given the single-pilot operation and relatively higher workload, they would be just as much at risk (possibly even more) to be involved in an accident than a commercial crew. Any fatigued person will exhibit the same problems: sleepiness, difficulty concentrating, apathy, feeling of isolation, annoyance, increased reaction time to stimulus, slowing of higher-level mental functioning, decreased vigilance, memory problems, task fixation, and increased errors while performing tasks.

None of these are good things to have happen to a pilot, much less if there is no one else in the aircraft to help out.

In a variety of studies, fatigued individuals consistently underreported how tired they really were, as measured by physiologic parameters. A tired individual truly does not realize the extent of actual impairment. No degree of experience, motivation, medication, coffee, or will power can overcome fatigue.

Antidote to Fatigue

Obtaining adequate sleep is the best way to prevent or resolve fatigue. Sleep provides the body with a period of rest and recuperation. Insufficient sleep will result in significant physical and psychological problems. On average, a healthy adult does best with eight hours of uninterrupted sleep, but significant personal variations occur. For example, increasing sleep difficulties occur as we age, with significant shortening of nighttime sleep. A variety of medical conditions can influence the quality and duration of sleep. To name a few: sleep apnea, restless leg syndrome, certain medications, depression, stress, insomnia, and chronic pain. Some of the more common social or behavioral issues are: late-night activities, excessive alcohol or caffeine use, travel, interpersonal strife, uncomfortable or unfamiliar surroundings, and shift work.

Prevention

No one is immune from fatigue. Yet, in our society, establishing widespread preventive measures to combat fatigue is often a very difficult goal to achieve. Individuals, as well as organizations, often ignore the problem until an accident occurs. Even then, implementing lasting change is not guaranteed. Lifestyle changes are not easy for individuals, particularly if that person isn't in complete control of the condition. For example, commercial pilots must contend with shift work and circadian rhythm disruption. Often, they also choose to commute long distances to work, so that by the time a work cycle starts they have already traveled for several hours. While a general aviation pilot may not have to deal with this, a busy lifestyle or other issues may lead to fatigue. Therefore, general aviation pilots must make every effort to modify personal lifestyle factors that cause fatigue.

Lifestyle Recommendations

Don't...

- Consume alcohol or caffeine 3-4 hours before going to bed.
- Eat a heavy meal just before bedtime.
- Take work to bed.
- Exercise 2-3 hours before bedtime. While working out promotes a healthy lifestyle, it shouldn't be done too close to bedtime.
- Use sleeping pills (prescription or otherwise).

Do...

- Be mindful of the side effects of certain medications, even over-the-counter medications — drowsiness or impaired alertness is a concern.
- Consult a physician to diagnose and treat any medical conditions causing sleep problems.
- Create a comfortable sleep environment at home. Adjust heating and cooling as needed. Get a comfortable mattress.
- When traveling, select hotels that provide a comfortable environment.
- Get into the habit of sleeping eight hours per night. When needed, and if possible, nap during the day, but limit the nap to less than 30 minutes. Longer naps produce sleep inertia, which is counterproductive.
- Try to turn in at the same time each day. This establishes a routine and helps you fall asleep quicker.
- If you can't fall asleep within 30 minutes of going to bed, get up and try an activity that helps induce sleep (watch non-violent TV, read, listen to relaxing music, etc.).
- Get plenty of rest and minimize stress before a flight. If problems preclude a good night's sleep, rethink the flight and postpone it accordingly.

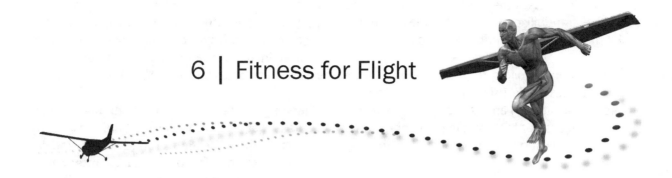

6 | Fitness for Flight

Medical Certification

All pilots except those flying gliders and free air balloons must possess valid medical certificates in order to exercise the privileges of their airman certificates. The periodic medical examinations required for medical certification are conducted by designated Aviation Medical Examiners, who are physicians with a special interest in aviation safety and training in aviation medicine.

The standards for medical certification are contained in 14 CFR Part 67. Pilots who have a history of certain medical conditions described in these standards are mandatorily disqualified from flying. These medical conditions include a personality disorder manifested by overt acts, a psychosis, alcoholism, drug dependence, epilepsy, an unexplained disturbance of consciousness, myocardial infarction, angina pectoris and diabetes requiring medication for its control. Other medical conditions may be temporarily disqualifying, such as acute infections, anemia, and peptic ulcer. Pilots who do not meet medical standards may still be qualified under special issuance provisions or the exemption process. This may require that either additional medical information be provided or practical flight tests be conducted.

Student pilots should visit an Aviation Medical Examiner as soon as possible in their flight training in order to avoid unnecessary training expenses should they not meet the medical standards. For the same reason, the student pilot who plans to enter commercial aviation should apply for the highest class of medical certificate that might be necessary in the pilot's career.

Caution

The CFRs prohibit a pilot who possesses a current medical certificate from performing crewmember duties while the pilot has a known medical condition or increase of a known medical condition that would make the pilot unable to meet the standards for the medical certificate.

Illness

Even a minor illness suffered in day-to-day living can seriously degrade performance of many piloting tasks vital to safe flight. Illness can produce fever and distracting symptoms that can impair judgment, memory, alertness, and the ability to make calculations. Although symptoms from an illness may be under adequate control with a medication, the medication itself may decrease pilot performance.

The safest rule is not to fly while suffering from any illness. If this rule is considered too stringent for a particular illness, the pilot should contact an Aviation Medical Examiner for advice.

Medication

Pilot performance can be seriously degraded by both prescribed and over-the-counter medications, as well as by the medical conditions for which they are taken. Many medications, such as tranquilizers, sedatives, strong pain relievers, and cough-suppressant preparations, have primary effects that may impair judgment, memory, alertness, coordination, vision, and the ability to make calculations. Others, such as antihistamines, blood pressure drugs, muscle relaxants, and agents to control diarrhea and motion sickness, have side effects that may impair the same critical functions. Any medication that depresses the nervous system, such as a sedative, tranquilizer or antihistamine, can make a pilot much more susceptible to hypoxia.

The CFRs prohibit pilots from performing crewmember duties while using any medication that affects the faculties in any way contrary to safety. The safest rule is not to fly as a crewmember while taking any medication, unless approved to do so by the FAA.

Stress

Stress from the pressures of everyday living can impair pilot performance, often in very subtle ways. Difficulties, particularly at work, can occupy thought processes enough to markedly decrease alertness. Distraction can so interfere with judgment that unwarranted risks are taken, such as flying into deteriorating weather conditions to keep on schedule. Stress and fatigue can be an extremely hazardous combination.

Most pilots do not leave stress "on the ground." Therefore, when more than usual difficulties are being experienced, a pilot should consider delaying flight until these difficulties are satisfactorily resolved.

Emotion

Certain emotionally-upsetting events, including a serious argument, death of a family member, separation or divorce, loss of job, and financial catastrophe, can render a pilot unable to fly an aircraft safely. The emotions of anger, depression, and anxiety from such events not only decrease alertness but also may lead to taking risks that border on self-destruction. Any pilot who experiences an emotionally upsetting event should not fly until satisfactorily recovered from it.

Effects of Altitude

Ear Block

As the aircraft cabin pressure decreases during ascent, the expanding air in the middle ear pushes the eustachian tube open, and by escaping down it to the nasal passages, equalizes in pressure with the cabin pressure. But during descent, the pilot must periodically open the eustachian tube to equalize

pressure. This can be accomplished by swallowing, yawning, tensing muscles in the throat, or if these do not work, by a combination of closing the mouth, pinching the nose closed, and attempting to blow through the nostrils (Valsalva maneuver).

Either an upper respiratory infection, such as a cold or sore throat, or a nasal allergic condition can produce enough congestion around the eustachian tube to make equalization difficult. Consequently, the difference in pressure between the middle ear and aircraft cabin can build up to a level that will hold the eustachian tube closed, making equalization difficult if not impossible. The problem is commonly referred to as an "ear block."

An ear block produces severe ear pain and loss of hearing that can last from several hours to several days. Rupture of the ear drum can occur in flight or after landing. Fluid can accumulate in the middle ear and become infected.

An ear block is prevented by not flying with an upper respiratory infection or nasal allergic condition. Adequate protection is usually not provided by decongestant sprays or drops to reduce congestion around the eustachian tubes. Oral decongestants have side effects that can significantly impair pilot performance.

If an ear block does not clear shortly after landing, a physician should be consulted.

Sinus Block

During ascent and descent, air pressure in the sinuses equalizes with the aircraft cabin pressure through small openings that connect the sinuses to the nasal passages. Either an upper respiratory infection, such as a cold or sinusitis, or a nasal allergic condition can produce enough congestion around an opening to slow equalization, and as the difference in pressure between the sinus and cabin mounts, eventually plug the opening. This "sinus block" occurs most frequently during descent.

A sinus block can occur in the frontal sinuses, located above each eyebrow, or in the maxillary sinuses, located in each upper cheek. It will usually produce excruciating pain over the sinus area. A maxillary sinus block can also make the upper teeth ache. Bloody mucus may discharge from the nasal passages.

A sinus block is prevented by not flying with an upper respiratory infection or nasal allergic condition. Adequate protection is usually not provided by decongestant sprays or drops to reduce congestion around the sinus openings. Oral decongestants have side effects that can impair pilot performance.

If a sinus block does not clear shortly after landing, a physician should be consulted.

Hyperventilation in Flight

Hyperventilation, or an abnormal increase in the volume of air breathed in and out of the lungs, can occur subconsciously when a stressful situation is encountered in flight. As hyperventilation "blows off" excessive carbon dioxide from the body, a pilot can experience symptoms of lightheadedness, suffocation, drowsiness, tingling in the extremities, and coolness and react to them with even greater hyperventilation. Incapacitation can eventually result from incoordination, disorientation, and painful muscle spasms. Finally, unconsciousness can occur.

The symptoms of hyperventilation subside within a few minutes after the rate and depth of breathing are consciously brought back under control. The buildup of carbon dioxide in the body can be hastened by controlled breathing in and out of a paper bag held over the nose and mouth.

Early symptoms of hyperventilation and hypoxia are similar. Moreover, hyperventilation and hypoxia can occur at the same time. Therefore, if a pilot is using an oxygen system when symptoms are experienced, the oxygen regulator should immediately be set to deliver 100 percent oxygen, and then the system checked to assure that it has been functioning effectively before giving attention to rate and depth of breathing.

Aerobatic Flight

Pilots planning to engage in aerobatics should be aware of the physiological stresses associated with accelerative forces during aerobatic maneuvers. Many prospective aerobatic trainees enthusiastically enter aerobatic instruction but find their first experiences with G forces to be unanticipated and very uncomfortable. To minimize or avoid potential adverse effects, the aerobatic instructor and trainee must have a basic understanding of the physiology of G force adaptation.

Forces experienced with a rapid push-over maneuver result in the blood and body organs being displaced toward the head. Depending on forces involved and individual tolerance, a pilot may experience discomfort, headache, "red-out," and even unconsciousness.

Forces experienced with a rapid pull-up maneuver result in the blood and body organ displacement toward the lower part of the body away from the head. Since the brain requires continuous blood circulation for an adequate oxygen supply, there is a physiologic limit to the time the pilot can tolerate higher forces before losing consciousness. As the blood circulation to the brain decreases as a result of forces involved, a pilot will experience "narrowing" of visual fields, "gray-out," "black- out," and unconsciousness. Even a brief loss of consciousness in a maneuver can lead to improper control movement causing structural failure of the aircraft or collision with another object or terrain.

In steep turns, the centrifugal forces tend to push the pilot into the seat, thereby resulting in blood and body organ displacement toward the lower part of the body as in the case of rapid pull-up maneuvers and with the same physiologic effects and symptoms.

Physiologically, humans progressively adapt to imposed strains and stress, and with practice, any maneuver will have decreasing effect. Tolerance to G forces is dependent on human physiology and the individual pilot. These factors include the skeletal anatomy, the cardiovascular architecture, the nervous system, the quality of the blood, the general physical state, and experience and recency of exposure. The pilot should consult an Aviation Medical

Examiner prior to aerobatic training and be aware that poor physical condition can reduce tolerance to accelerative forces.

The above information provides pilots with a brief summary of the physiologic effects of G forces. It does not address methods of "counteracting" these effects. There are numerous references on the subject of G forces during aerobatics available to pilots. Among these are "G Effects on the Pilot During Aerobatics," FAA-AM-72-28, and "G Incapacitation in Aerobatic Pilots: A Flight Hazard" FAA-AM-82-13. These are available from the National Technical Information Service, Springfield, Virginia 22161.

Reference: FAA AC 91-61, "A Hazard in Aerobatics: Effects of G-forces on Pilots."

Judgment Aspects of Collision Avoidance

Determining Relative Altitude. Use the horizon as a reference point. If the other aircraft is above the horizon, it is probably on a higher flight path. If the aircraft appears to be below the horizon, it is probably flying at a lower altitude.

Taking Appropriate Action. Pilots should be familiar with rules on right-of-way, so if an aircraft is on an obvious collision course, one can take immediate evasive action, preferably in compliance with applicable Federal Aviation Regulations.

Consider Multiple Threats. The decision to climb, descend, or turn is a matter of personal judgment, but one should anticipate that the other pilot may also be making a quick maneuver. Watch the other aircraft during the maneuver and begin your scanning again immediately since there may be other aircraft in the area.

Collision Course Targets. Any aircraft that appears to have no relative motion and stays in one scan quadrant is likely to be on a collision course. Also, if a target shows no lateral or vertical motion, but increases in size, take evasive action.

Recognize High Hazard Areas

Airways, especially near VORs, and Class B, Class C, Class D, and Class E surface areas are places where aircraft tend to cluster.

Remember, most collisions occur during days when the weather is good. Being in a "radar environment" still requires vigilance to avoid collisions.

Cockpit Management. Studying maps, checklists, and manuals before flight, with other proper preflight planning; e.g., noting necessary radio frequencies and organizing cockpit materials, can reduce the amount of time required to look at these items during flight, permitting more scan time.

Windshield Conditions. Dirty or bug-smeared windshields can greatly reduce the ability of pilots to see other aircraft. Keep a clean windshield.

Visibility Conditions. Smoke, haze, dust, rain, and flying towards the sun can also greatly reduce the ability to detect targets.

Visual Obstructions in the Cockpit

Pilots need to move their heads to see around blind spots caused by fixed aircraft structures, such as door posts, wings, etc. It will be necessary at times to maneuver the aircraft; e.g., lift a wing, to facilitate seeing.

Pilots must ensure curtains and other cockpit objects (e.g., maps on glare shield), are removed and stowed during flight.

Lights On

Day or night, use of exterior lights can greatly increase the conspicuity of any aircraft.

Keep interior lights low at night.

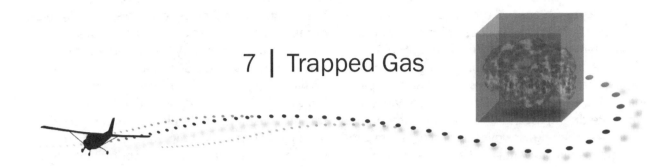

7 | Trapped Gas

As we ascend in the atmosphere, barometric pressure falls from 760 mmHg at sea level, to approximately 550 mmHg at 7,000 feet, and 380 mmHg at 18,000 feet. The resultant fall of barometric pressure to half that of sea level will proportionally cause any gas to expand to double the volume at the same temperature (Dalton's Law). This creates the potential for expansion of trapped gas within the human body, which maintains a constant temperature of 37 degrees Centigrade.

Virtually all areas where gas can be trapped in the human body are normally able to ventilate, but under abnormal physiologic conditions the ability to ventilate can become lost and create a problem in flight. Trauma and medical intervention may introduce gas into the human body. Trapped gas is defined as any gas within the human body that is unable to communicate with the external world. Thus gas within the lungs is not trapped. Gas within the stomach and gastrointestinal tract, however, has the potential to become trapped through function of peristalsis and external compression. The most common anatomical areas affected are the middle ear and sinuses.

The sinuses are able under normal conditions to passively ventilate through their ostia. Ventilation of the middle ear, connected to the pharynx by the eustachian tube, is controlled by a flutter valve. This valve allows expansion of air within the middle ear to spontaneously ventilate and be expelled into the pharynx. [Figure 7.1] Thus on ascent, as barometric pressure drops, gas trapped within the middle ear should ventilate spontaneously. However, on decent, as barometric pressure drops, and the relative pressure within the middle ear, as opposed to the external ear across the tympanic membrane,

will be much lower, and the tympanic membrane may bow inward. Relief of this bowing may require active ventilation of the middle ear through contraction of the levator palatini and tensor palatini muscles. This can be performed by yawning or with the Valsalva maneuver, where in the nasopharyngeal pressure is increased against a closed eustachian orifice while compressing the nares. A modified Valsalva is performed by swallowing while holding the nose closed. Additionally the Frenzel maneuver may be performed, thrusting the jaw forward and opening the eustachian tube. Aeration of the middle ear also permits passive ventilation of the communicating mastoid air cells.

Middle Ear Anatomy

In the event of a respiratory infection the eustachian tube may become compromised due to edema, and gas in the middle ear becomes trapped. If air is unable to escape, or more commonly, unable to re-ventilate the middle ear on descent, significant pain will result as the tympanic membrane is

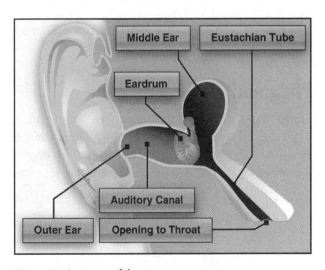

Figure 7.1 Anatomy of the ear.

contracted inward. Eventually, if unrelieved, the tympanic membrane will rupture and equalize the pressure. This rupture, while seemingly catastrophic, will typically heal without treatment in 2 to 3 weeks. A similar condition can occur when a respiratory infection compromises the ostia of the paranasal sinuses; the sinus will tend to spontaneously ventilate during ascent as air escapes through the narrowed opening. However, on descent there is insufficient ability to ventilate the sinuses and the result is exquisite pain and occasionally hemorrhage into the sinus. Other types of barotraumas occur, including rupture of the round or oval windows of the inner ear, causing perilymph fistula, infections, and in some cases, an onset of ear pain many hours later, known as a delayed ear block.

Delayed ear block occurs after breathing 100% oxygen in flight. By the time the aviator lands, the middle ear air containing 21% oxygen, has been fully replaced with 100% oxygen. The resulting metabolism of the oxygen by middle ear mucosal cells can produce a relative vacuum some hours later. While painful, it can be relieved by ventilating the ear. In fact, it can be prevented by ventilating the ear several times after landing, thereby returning the gas mixture to normal.

Bacterial infections within the teeth can result in gas formation with potential trapping. This is typically from pulpitis or a significant abscess, although occasionally gas may be trapped under a crown or occur acutely following dental surgery. Trapped dental gas can cause significant pain on ascent, which is usually relieved upon descent. Gas may become trapped in the lungs, where villi may fail to ventilate and spontaneously rupture. This may result in a catastrophic pneumothorax.

Pneumothorax

Trapped gas within the gastrointestinal tract is usually relieved by belching or passing flatus. Failure to do so may result in significant stretching of the intestinal contents, causing pain. Only in rare cases,

such as a weakened diverticulum of the colon, does bowel rupture occur due to gas trapping. Surgical or medical procedures may introduce gas into the vitreous humor of the eye or into the cerebrospinal fluid of the brain. Such gas, when expanding on flight, may cause a fatal vasovagal syncope. Any individual with retained gas within the eye or central nervous system should be strictly forbidden from flying until it is completely reabsorbed. Post-surgical retained gas within the abdominal cavity is a relatively minor problem and the individual can be permitted to fly at the discretion of the treating surgeon.

The major implications of trapped gas within the body from a pilot's point of view are interference with the pilot's ability to function properly and concentrate on operating the aircraft. The most common barotraumas involving pilots are an ear or sinus block with severe pain while flying. The pain may be sufficient enough to completely distract the pilot from operating the aircraft, resulting in loss of control. Educating pilots not to fly with a cold is the most effective preventative measure. Occasionally it is necessary for a pilot to carry topical decongestant sprays, such as Neo-Synephrine, capable of opening edematous passageways and permitting equilibration of pressure. It must be emphasized that decongestants should only be used in an emergency. Chronic use of such medications results in a rebound phenomena of rhinitis medicamosa, where repeated use of decongestant sprays are required to maintain a semblance of normal activity in an otherwise unaffected nasal airway. In an emergency, a myringotomy may be required to relieve pressure in the middle ear. These can be expected to heal without complications in two to three weeks.

Reference: Yarington CT, Hanna HH, Otolaryngology in Aerospace Medicine, in Fundamentals of Aerospace Medicine Chapter 15, 567-92, and Fundamentals of Aerospace Medicine, 3rd Edition, DeHart and Davis, 2002.

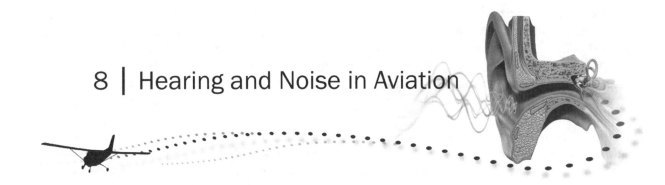

8 | Hearing and Noise in Aviation

Hearing

The term *hearing* describes the process, function, or power of perceiving sound. Hearing is second only to vision as a physiological sensory mechanism to obtain critical information during the operation of an aircraft. The sense of hearing makes it possible to perceive, process, and identify among the myriad of sounds from the surrounding environment.

Anatomy and Physiology of the Auditory System

The auditory system consists of the external ear, ear canal, eardrum, auditory ossicles, cochlea (which resembles a snail shell and is filled with fluid), and the auditory nerve. [Figure 8.1]

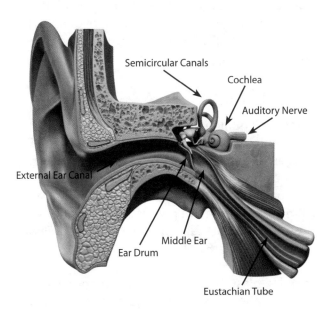

Figure. 8.1 Anatomy of the auditory system.

Ambient sound waves are collected by the external ear, conducted through the ear canal, and cause the eardrum to vibrate. Eardrum vibration is mechanically transmitted to the ossicles, which, in turn, produce vibration of a flexible window in the cochlea. This vibration causes a pressure wave in the fluid located inside the cochlea, moving thousands of hair-like sensory receptors lining the inner walls of the cochlea. The movement of these receptors resembles the gentle movement of a crop field caused by the wind. The stimulation of these sensors produces an electrical signal that is transmitted to the brain by the auditory nerve. This signal is then processed by the brain and identified as a particular type of sound.

Sound

The term *sound* is used to describe the mechanical radiant energy that is transmitted by longitudinal pressure waves in a medium (solid, liquid, or gas). Sound waves are variations in air pressures above and below the ambient pressure. From a more practical point of view, this term describes the sensation perceived by the sense of hearing. All sounds have three distinctive variables: frequency, intensity, and duration.

Frequency. This is the physical property of sound that gives it a pitch. Since sound energy propagates in a wave-form, it can be measured in terms of wave oscillations or wave cycles per second, known as hertz (Hz). Sounds that are audible to the human ear fall in the frequency range of about 20–20,000 Hz, and the highest sensitivity is between 500 and 4,000 Hz. Sounds below 20 Hz and above 20,000 Hz cannot be perceived by the human ear. Normal conversation takes place in the frequency range from 500 to 3,000 Hz.

Intensity. This is the correlation between sound intensity and loudness. The decibel (dB) is the unit used to measure sound intensity. The range of normal hearing sensitivity of the human ear is between -10 to +25 dB. Sounds below -10 dB are generally imperceptible. A pilot who cannot hear a sound unless its intensity is higher than 25 dB (at any frequency) is already experiencing hearing loss.

Duration. This determines the quality of the perception and discrimination of a sound, as well as the potential risk of hearing impairment when exposed to high intensity sounds. The adverse consequences of a short-duration exposure to a loud sound can be as bad as a long-duration exposure to a less intense sound. Therefore, the potential for causing hearing damage is determined not only by the duration of a sound but also by its intensity.

Noise

The term *noise* refers to a sound, especially one which lacks agreeable musical quality, is noticeably unpleasant, or is too loud. In other words, noise is any unwanted or annoying sound. Categorizing a sound as noise can be very subjective. For example, loud rock music can be described as an enjoyable sound by some (usually teenagers), and at the same time described as noise by others (usually adults). [Figure 8.2]

Sources	Level (dB)
Whispered voice	20-30
Urban home, average office	40-60
Average male conversation	60-65
Noisy office, low traffic street	60-80
Jet transports (cabin)	60-88
Small single plane (cockpit)	70-90
Public address (PA) systems	90-100
Busy city street	80-100
Single rotor helicopter (cockpit)	80-102
Power lawnmower, chainsaw	100-110
Snowmobile, thunder	110-120
Rock concert	115-120
Jet engine (proximity)	130-160

Figure 8.2 Sources of sound/noise.

Sources of Noise in Aviation. The aviation environment is characterized by multiple sources of noise, both on the ground and in the air. Exposure of pilots to noise became an issue following the introduction of the first powered aircraft by the Wright Brothers, and has been a prevalent problem ever since. Noise is produced by aircraft equipment powerplants, transmission systems, jet efflux, propellers, rotors, hydraulic and electrical actuators, cabin conditioning and pressurization systems, cockpit advisory and alert systems, communications equipment, etc. Noise can also be caused by the aerodynamic interaction between ambient air (boundary layer) and the surface of the aircraft fuselage, wings, control surfaces, and landing gear. These auditory inputs allow pilots to assess and monitor the operational status of their aircraft. All pilots know the sounds of a normal-functioning aircraft. On the other hand, unexpected sounds or the lack of them, may alert pilots to possible malfunctions, failures, or hazards. Every pilot has experienced a cockpit or cabin environment that was so loud that it was necessary to shout to be heard. These sounds not only make the work environment more stressful but can, over time, cause permanent hearing impairment. However, it is also important to remember that individual exposure to noise is a common occurrence away from the aviation working environment—at home or work, on the road, and in public areas. The effects of pre-flight exposure to noise can adversely affect pilot in-flight performance.

Types of Noise

Steady. Continuous noise of sudden or gradual onset and long duration (more than 1 second). Examples: aircraft powerplant noise, propeller noise, and pressurization system noise. According to the Occupational Safety and Health Administration (OSHA), the maximum permissible continuous exposure level to steady noise in a working environment is 90 dB for 8 hours.

Impulse/blast. Noise pulses of sudden onset and brief duration (less than 1 second) that usually exceed an intensity of 140 dB. Examples: firing a handgun, detonating a firecracker, backfiring of a piston engine, high-volume squelching of radio equipment, and a sonic boom caused by breaking the sound barrier. The eardrum may be ruptured by intense levels (140 dB) of impulse/blast noise.

Effects of Noise Exposure

Physiologic

Ear discomfort. May occur during exposure to a 120 dB noise.

Ear pain. May occur during exposure to a 130 dB noise.

Eardrum rupture. May occur during exposure to a 140 dB) noise.

Temporary hearing impairment. Unprotected exposure to loud, steady noise over 90 dB for a short time, even several hours, may cause hearing impairment. This effect is usually temporary and hearing returns to normal within several hours following cessation of the noise exposure.

Permanent hearing impairment. Unprotected exposure to loud noise (higher than 90 dB) for eight or more hours per day for several years, may cause a permanent hearing loss. Permanent hearing impairment occurs initially in the vicinity of 4,000 Hz (outside the conversational range) and can go unnoticed by the individual for some time. It is also important to remember that hearing sensitivity normally decreases as a function of age at frequencies from 1,000 to 6,000 Hz, beginning around age 30.

Psychologic

Subjective effects. Annoying high-intensity noise can cause distraction, fatigue, irritability, startle responses, sudden awakening and poor sleep quality, loss of appetite, headache, vertigo, nausea, and impair concentration and memory.

Speech interference. Loud noise can interfere with or mask normal speech, making it difficult to understand.

Performance. Noise is a distraction and can increase the number of errors in any given task. Tasks that require vigilance, concentration, calculations, and making judgments about time can be adversely affected by exposure to loud noise higher than 90 dB.

How to Protect Your Hearing

Limiting duration of exposure to noise. OSHA established permissible noise exposure limits for the workplace (including the cockpit of an aircraft): [Figure 8.3]

Noise Intensity (dB)	Exposure Limit (hours per day)
90	8
92	6
95	4
97	3
100	2
102	1.5
105	1
110	.5
115	.25

Figure 8.3 Noise exposure level limits.

Use Hearing Protection Equipment. If the ambient noise level exceeds OSHA's permissible noise exposure limits, you should use hearing protection devices—earplugs, earmuffs, communication headsets, or active noise reduction headsets. Even if an individual already has some level of permanent hearing loss, using hearing protection equipment should prevent further hearing damage. These protection devices attenuate noise waves before they reach the eardrum, and most of them are effective at reducing high-frequency noise levels above 1,000 Hz. It is very important to emphasize that the use of these devices does not interfere with speech communications during flight because they reduce high-frequency background noise, making speech signals clearer and more comprehensible.

Earplugs. Insertable-type earplugs offer a very popular, inexpensive, effective, and comfortable approach to provide hearing protection. To be effective, earplugs must be inserted properly to create an airtight seal in the ear canal. The wax-impregnated moldable polyurethane earplugs provide an effective universal fit for all users and provide 30 to 35 dB of noise protection across all frequency bands.

Communication headsets. In general, headsets provide the same level of noise attenuation as earmuffs, and are also more easily donned and removed that earplugs, but the microphone can interfere with the donning of an oxygen mask.

Active noise reduction headsets. This type of headset uses active noise reduction technology that allows the manipulation of sound and signal waves to reduce noise, improve signal-to-noise ratios, and enhance sound quality. Active noise reduction provides effective protection against low frequency noise. The electronic coupling of a low frequency noise wave with its exact mirror image cancels this noise.

Combinations of protection devices. The combination of earplugs with earmuffs or communication headsets is recommended when ambient noise levels are above 115 dB. Earplugs, combined with active noise reduction headsets, provide the maximum level of individual hearing protection that can be achieved with current technology.

Summary

- Hearing is second only to vision as a sensory mechanism to obtain critical information during the operation of an aircraft.
- All sounds have three distinctive variables: frequency, intensity, and duration.
- Normal conversation takes place in the frequency range from 500 to 3,000 Hz.
- Daily exposure to noise levels higher than 90 dB can cause hearing impairment. This can go unnoticed initially because it occurs in the vicinity of 4,000 Hz (outside the conversational range)
- If the ambient noise level reaches 90 dB, you must use hearing protection equipment to prevent hearing impairment.
- Exposure to loud noise before flying (at home, while driving, at a party, etc.) can be as harmful as exposure to aircraft noise.

9 | Altitude-Induced Decompression Sickness

Tiny Bubbles, BIG Troubles

Decompression sickness (DCS) describes a condition characterized by a variety of symptoms resulting from exposure to low barometric pressures that cause inert gases (mainly nitrogen), normally dissolved in body fluids and tissues, to come out of physical solution and form bubbles. DCS can occur during exposure to altitude (altitude DCS) or during ascent from depth (mining or diving). The first documented cases of DCS (Caisson Disease) were reported in 1841 by a mining engineer who observed the occurrence of pain and muscle cramps among coal miners exposed to air-pressurized mine shafts designed to keep water out. The first description of a case resulting from diving activities while wearing a pressurized hard hat was reported in 1869.

Altitude-Induced Decompression Sickness

Altitude DCS became a commonly observed problem associated with high-altitude balloon and aircraft flights in the 1930s. In present-day aviation, technology allows civilian aircraft (commercial and private) to fly higher and faster than ever before. Though modern aircraft are safer and more reliable, occupants are still subject to the stresses of high altitude flight—and the unique problems that go with these lofty heights. A century and one-half after the first DCS case was described, our understanding of DCS has improved, and a body of knowledge has accumulated; however, this problem is far from being solved. Altitude DCS still represents a risk to the occupants of modern aircraft.

Tiny Bubbles

According to Henry's Law, when the pressure of a gas over a liquid is decreased, the amount of gas dissolved in that liquid will also decrease. One of the best practical demonstrations of this law is offered by opening a soft drink. When the cap is removed from the bottle, gas is heard escaping, and bubbles can be seen forming in the soda. This is carbon dioxide gas coming out of solution as a result of sudden exposure to lower barometric pressure. Similarly, nitrogen is an inert gas normally stored throughout the human body (tissues and fluids) in physical solution. When the body is exposed to decreased barometric pressures (as in flying an unpressurized aircraft to altitude, or during a rapid decompression), the nitrogen dissolved in the body comes out of solution. If the nitrogen is forced to leave the solution too rapidly, bubbles form in different areas of the body, causing a variety of signs and symptoms. The most common symptom is joint pain, which is known as "the bends."

Trouble Sites

Although bubbles can form anywhere in the body, the most frequently targeted anatomic locations are the shoulders, elbows, knees, and ankles.

Figure 9.1 lists the different DCS types with their corresponding bubble formation sites and their most common symptoms. "The bends" (joint pain) account for about 60 to 70% of all altitude DCS cases, with the shoulder being the most common site. Neurologic manifestations are present in about 10 to 15% of all DCS cases, with headache and visual disturbances being the most common symptoms. "The chokes" are very infrequent and occur in less than 2% of all DCS cases. Skin manifestations are present in about 10 to 15% of all DCS cases.

Medical Treatment

Mild cases of "the bends" and skin bends (excluding mottled or marbled skin appearance) may disappear during descent from high altitude, but still require medical evaluation. If the signs and symptoms persist during descent or reappear at ground level, it is necessary to provide hyperbaric oxygen treatment immediately (100% oxygen delivered in a high-pressure chamber). Neurological DCS, "the chokes," and skin bends with mottled or marbled skin lesions [Figure 9.1] should always be treated with hyperbaric oxygenation. These conditions are very serious and potentially fatal if untreated.

Facts About Breathing 100% Oxygen

One of the most significant breakthroughs in altitude DCS research was the discovery that breathing 100% oxygen before exposure to a low barometric pressure (oxygen prebreathing), decreases the risk of developing altitude DCS. Oxygen prebreathing promotes the elimination (washout) of nitrogen from body tissues. Prebreathing 100% oxygen for 30 minutes prior to initiating ascent to altitude reduces the risk of altitude DCS for short exposures (10–30 minutes only) to altitudes between 18,000 and 43,000 feet. However, oxygen prebreathing has to be continued, without interruption, with inflight 100% oxygen breathing to provide effective protection against altitude DCS. Furthermore, it is very important to understand that breathing 100% oxygen only during flight (ascent, enroute, descent) does not decrease the risk of altitude DCS and should not be used in lieu of oxygen prebreathing.

Although 100% oxygen prebreathing is an effective method to provide individual protection against altitude DCS, it is not a logistically simple or an inexpensive approach for the protection of civil aviation flyers (commercial or private). Therefore, at the present time, it is only used by military flight crews and astronauts for their protection during high altitude and space operations.

Predisposing Factors

Altitude

There is no specific altitude that can be considered an absolute altitude exposure threshold, below which it can be assured that no one will develop altitude DCS. However, there is very little evidence of altitude DCS occurring among healthy individuals at altitudes below 18,000 feet who have not been SCUBA (Self Contained Underwater Breathing Apparatus) diving. Individual exposures to altitudes between 18,000 feet and 25,000 feet have shown a low occurrence of altitude DCS. Most cases of altitude DCS occur among individuals exposed to altitudes of 25,000 feet or higher. A US Air Force study of altitude DCS cases reported that only 13% occurred below 25,000 feet. The higher the altitude of exposure, the greater the risk of developing altitude DCS. It is important to clarify that although exposures to incremental altitudes above 18,000 feet show an incremental risk of altitude DCS, they do not show a direct relationship with the severity of the various types of DCS. [Figure 9.1]

Repetitive Exposures

Repetitive exposures to altitudes above 18,000 feet within a short period of time (a few hours) also increase the risk of developing altitude DCS.

Rate of Ascent

The faster the rate of ascent to altitude, the greater the risk of developing altitude DCS. An individual exposed to a rapid decompression (high rate of ascent) above 18,000 feet has a greater risk of altitude DCS than being exposed to the same altitude but at a lower rate of ascent.

Time at Altitude

The longer the duration of the exposure to altitudes of 18,000 feet and above, the greater the risk of altitude DCS.

Age

There are some reports indicating a higher risk of altitude DCS with increasing age.

Previous Injury

There is some indication that recent joint or limb injuries may predispose individuals to developing "the bends."

DCS Type	Bubble Location	Signs & Symptoms (Clinical Manifestations)
BENDS	Mostly large joints of the body (elbows, shoulders, hip, wrists, knees, ankles)	• Localized deep pain, ranging from mild (a "niggle") to excruciating. Sometimes a dull ache, but rarely a sharp pain. • Active and passive motion of the joint aggravates the pain. • Pain can occur at altitude, during the descent, or many hours later.
NEUROLOGIC Manifestations	Brain	• Confusion or memory loss • Headache • Spots in visual field (scotoma), tunnel vision, double vision (diplopia), or blurry vision • Unexplained extreme fatigue or behavior changes • Seizures, dizziness, vertigo, nausea, vomiting and unconsciousness may occur
	Spinal Cord	• Abnormal sensations such as burning, stinging, and tingling around the lower chest and back • Symptoms may spread from the feet up and may be accompanied by ascending weakness or paralysis • Girdling abdominal or chest pain
	Peripheral Nerves	• Urinary and rectal incontinence • Abnormal sensations, such as numbness, burning, stinging and tingling (paresthesia) • Muscle weakness or twitching
CHOKES	Lungs	• Burning deep chest pain (under the sternum) • Pain is aggravated by breathing • Shortness of breath (dyspnea) • Dry constant cough
SKIN BENDS	Skin	• Itching usually around the ears, face, neck arms, and upper torso • Sensation of tiny insects crawling over the skin • Mottled or marbled skin usually around the shoulders, upper chest and abdomen, accompanied by itching • Swelling of the skin, accompanied by tiny scar-like skin depressions (pitting edema)

Figure 9.1 Signs and symptoms of altitude decompression sickness.

Ambient Temperature

There is some evidence suggesting that individual exposure to very cold ambient temperatures may increase the risk of altitude DCS.

Body Type

Typically, a person who has a high body fat content is at greater risk of altitude DCS. Due to poor blood supply, nitrogen is stored in greater amounts in fat tissues. Although fat represents only 15% of an adult normal body, it stores over half of the total amount of nitrogen (about 1 liter) normally dissolved in the body.

Exercise

When a person is physically active while flying at altitudes above 18,000 feet, there is greater risk of altitude DCS.

Alcohol Consumption

The after-effects of alcohol consumption increase the susceptibility to DCS.

Scuba Diving Before Flying

SCUBA diving requires breathing air under high pressure. Under these conditions, there is a significant increase in the amount of nitrogen dissolved in the body (body nitrogen saturation). The deeper the SCUBA dive, the greater the rate of body nitrogen saturation. Furthermore, SCUBA diving in high elevations (mountain lakes), at any given depth, results in greater body nitrogen saturation when compared to SCUBA diving at sea level at the same depth. Following SCUBA diving, if not enough time is allowed to eliminate the excess nitrogen stored in the body, altitude DCS can occur during exposure to altitudes as low as 5,000 feet or less.

What to do When Altitude DCS Occurs

- Put on your oxygen mask immediately and switch the regulator to 100% oxygen.
- Begin an emergency descent and land as soon as possible. Even if the symptoms disappear during descent, you should still land and seek medical evaluation while continuing to breathe oxygen.

- If one of your symptoms is joint pain, keep the affected area still; do not try to work pain out by moving the joint around.
- Upon landing seek medical assistance from an FAA medical officer, aviation medical examiner (AME) military flight surgeon, or a hyperbaric medicine specialist. Be aware that a physician not specialized in aviation or hypobaric medicine may not be familiar with this type of medical problem. Therefore, be your own advocate.
- Definitive medical treatment may involve the use of a hyperbaric chamber operated by specially trained personnel.
- Delayed signs and symptoms of altitude DCS can occur after return to ground level whether or not they were present during flight.

Things to Remember

- Altitude DCS is a risk every time you fly in an unpressurized aircraft above 18,000 feet (or at lower altitude if you SCUBA dive prior to the flight).
- Be familiar with the signs and symptoms of altitude DCS [Figure 9.1] and monitor all aircraft occupants, including yourself, any time you fly an unpressurized aircraft above 18,000 feet.
- Avoid unnecessary strenuous physical activity prior to flying an unpressurized aircraft above 18,000 feet and for 24 hours after the flight.
- Even if you are flying a pressurized aircraft, altitude DCS can occur as a result of sudden loss of cabin pressure (inflight rapid decompression).
- Following exposure to an inflight rapid decompressions do not fly for at least 24 hours. In the meantime, remain vigilant for the possible onset of delayed symptoms or signs of altitude DCS. If you present delayed symptoms or signs of altitude DCS, seek medical attention immediately.
- Keep in mind that breathing 100% oxygen during flight (ascent, enroute, descent) without oxygen prebreathing prior to take off does not prevent the occurrence of altitude DCS.
- Do not ignore any symptoms or signs that go away during the descent. In fact, this could confirm that you are actually suffering altitude

DCS. You should be medically evaluated as soon as possible.

- If there is any indication that you may have experienced altitude DCS, do not fly again until you are cleared to do so by an FAA medical officer, an aviation medical examiner, a military flight surgeon, or a hyperbaric medicine specialist.
- Allow at least 24 hours to elapse between SCUBA diving and flying.
- Be prepared for a future emergency by familiarizing yourself with the availability of hyperbaric chambers in your area of operations. However, keep in mind that not all of the available hyperbaric treatment facilities have personnel qualified to handle altitude DCS emergencies. To obtain information on the locations of hyperbaric treatment facilities capable of handling altitude DCS emergencies, call the Diver's Alert Network at (919) 684-8111.

For More Information

If you are interested in learning more about altitude DCS, as well as the other stressors that may affect your performance and/or your health during flight, we encourage you to enroll in the Physiological Training Course offered by the Aeromedical Education Division (Airman Education Programs) at the FAA Civil Aerospace Medical Institute in Oklahoma City. A similar course is also available at U.S. military physiological training facilities around the country through an FAA/DOD Training Agreement. For more information about any of these courses, call (405) 954-4837.

10 | Hypoxia: The Higher You Fly...
The Less Air in the Sky

Breathing is one of the most automatic things we do—over 20,000 times a day. Each breath does two things for our body. It expels carbon dioxide when we exhale, and takes in oxygen when we inhale. It's a delicate balance.

Exercise or stress increases the production of carbon dioxide, so we breathe faster to eliminate it and take in more oxygen at a greater rate.

Because of the effects of gravity, the amount of air containing oxygen is greater at sea level. For example, the pressure at sea level is twice that found at 18,000 feet MSL. Although the percentage of oxygen contained in air at 18,000 feet is identical to that at sea level (a little over 20%), the amount of air our lungs take in with each breath contains half the oxygen found at sea level. Breathing faster or more deeply doesn't help. In fact, because you're consciously over-riding a system that is normally automatic, you'll be compounding the problem by exhaling too much carbon dioxide.

Supplemental Oxygen

The solution is simple, familiar to most pilots, and required by FAR 91.211: supplemental oxygen. This regulation specifies a 30-minute limit before oxygen is required on flights between 12,500 and 14,000 feet MSL, and immediately upon exposure to cabin pressures above 14,000 feet MSL. For best protection, you are encouraged to use supplemental oxygen above 10,000 feet MSL.

At night, because vision is particularly sensitive to diminished oxygen, a prudent rule is to use supplemental oxygen when flying above 6,000 feet MSL.

So, when you fly at high altitudes, supplemental oxygen is the only solution. That's because supplemental oxygen satisfies the twin demands of having enough oxygen to meet your body's demands and a breathing rate that excretes the right amount of carbon dioxide.

Hypoxia

Unfortunately, our body doesn't give us reliable signals at the onset of hypoxia—oxygen starvation—unless we have received special training to recognize the symptoms. In fact, it's quite the contrary. The brain is the first part of the body to reflect a diminished oxygen supply, and the evidence of that is usually a loss of judgment.

Hypoxia Tests

Altitude chamber tests, in which high altitude flight conditions are duplicated, have shown that some people in an oxygen deficient environment actually experience a sense of euphoria—a feeling of increased well-being. These subjects can't write their name intelligibly, or even sort a deck of cards by suits…yet, they think they're doing just fine!

Such is the insidious nature of oxygen deprivation. It sneaks up on the unwary and steals the first line of sensory protection—the sense that something is wrong—dreadfully wrong.

The Higher You Go

Bear in mind, the progressive reduction of oxygen per breath will continue the higher you go. Flying above a layer of clouds that doesn't look too high, or flying in the mountains on a clear day—are the very environments that have caused many good "flat-land" pilots to get into trouble.

Symptoms

Everyone's response to hypoxia varies. Unless, as we've stated, you've had special training to recognize its symptoms, hypoxia doesn't give you much warning. It steals up on you, giving your body subtle clues. The order of symptoms varies among individuals: increased breathing rate, headache, lightheadedness, dizziness, tingling or warm sensations, sweating, poor coordination, impaired judgment, tunnel vision, and euphoria. Unless detected early and dealt with, hypoxia can be a real killer.

Caution and Safety

So, don't decide you'll try to fly over that range of mountains, thinking you'll turn back if you start to feel badly. You may feel great...until it's too late! Use supplemental oxygen.

Smoking and Altitude

A Western state pilot lived to tell about this one. Cruising at 13,500 feet MSL over mountainous terrain in his light single, he took a deep drag on his cigarette and next remembered being in a screaming dive with just enough altitude left in which to pull out! That deep drag replaced precious oxygen in his brain with carbon monoxide...and he passed out.

Briefly...

- When you breathe, you inhale oxygen and exhale carbon dioxide.
- With each normal breath, you inhale about one-half liter of air, 20% of which is oxygen.
- At 18,000' MSL, you have half the sea level air pressure; hence, only half the oxygen.
- Oxygen starvation first affects the brain; judgment is impaired, so you may not know you are in trouble.
- We all react differently to the effects of hypoxia. Only physiological training can safely "break the code" for you.

Physiological Training for Pilots

The effects of hypoxia can be safely experienced under professional supervision at the Civil Aeromedical Institute's altitude chamber in Oklahoma City and at 14 cooperating military installations throughout the U.S. If you would like to attend a one-day physiological training course, ask your FAA Accident Prevention Specialist for AC Form 3150-7.

You'll learn to recognize your symptoms of hypoxia. It could mean the difference between life and death.

11 | Sunglasses for Pilots: Beyond the Image

Sunglasses help safeguard a pilot's most important sensory asset — vision. A quality pair of sunglasses is essential in the cockpit environment to optimize visual performance. Sunglasses reduce the effects of harsh sunlight, decrease eye fatigue, and protect ocular tissues from exposure to harmful solar radiation. Additionally, they protect the pilot's eyes from impact with objects (i.e., flying debris from a bird strike, sudden decompression, or aerobatic maneuvers). Sunglasses can also aid the dark adaptation process, which is delayed by prolonged exposure to bright sunlight.

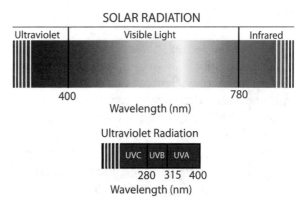

Figure 11.1 Electromagnetic radiation spectrum including visible, infrared, UVA, UVB, and UVC wavelengths.

Radiation

Radiation from the sun can damage skin and eyes when exposure is excessive or too intense. Fortunately, the Earth's atmosphere shelters us from the more hazardous solar radiation (i.e., gamma and X-ray); however, both infrared and ultraviolet radiation are present in our environment in varying amounts. This is dependant upon factors such as the time of day and year, latitude, altitude, weather conditions, and the reflectivity of surrounding surfaces. For example, exposure to ultraviolet radiation increases by approximately 5 percent for every 1,000 feet of altitude.

Atmospheric infrared energy consists of long-wavelength radiation (780 to 1400 nanometers [nm], see Figure 11.1). The warmth felt from the sun is provided by infrared radiation and is thought to be harmless to the skin and eyes at normal atmospheric exposure levels. More hazardous to human tissues is short-wavelength ultraviolet radiation. Ultraviolet is divided into three bandwidths: UVA (400 – 315 nm), UVB (315–280 nm), and UVC (<280 nm).[1] Excessive or chronic exposure to UVA and, to a greater extent, UVB, can cause sunburn, skin cancers, and is implicated in the formation of cataracts, macular degeneration, and other eye maladies.

The American Optometric Association recommends wearing sunglasses that incorporate 99 – 100% UVA and UVB protection. Fortunately, UVC, the most harmful form of ultraviolet radiation, is absorbed by the atmosphere's ozone layer before it reaches the Earth's surface. Some scientists believe, however, that depletion of the ozone layer may allow more ultraviolet to pass through the atmosphere,[2] making 100% ultraviolet protection a wise choice when selecting eyewear.

Lens Material

The three most common lens materials in use today are optical quality "crown" glass, monomer plastic (CR-39®), and polycarbonate plastic (see Figure 11.3). Lenses made from crown glass provide excellent optical properties (as indicated by the high Abbe value). Crown glass is more scratch-resistant but heavier and less impact-resistant than plastic. Glass absorbs some ultraviolet light; however, absorption is improved by adding certain chemicals during the manufacturing process or by applying a special coating. Glass retains tints best over time; however, for higher refractive correction, the color

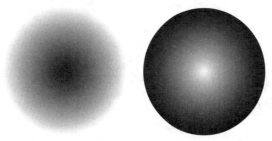

Figure 11.2 Illustration of non-uniform tints with glass lenses for high hyperopic (left) and myopic (right) corrections.

may be less uniform, as parts of the lens will be thicker than others. [Figure 11.2]

CR-39® plastic lenses possess excellent optical qualities, are lighter in weight, and more impact-resistant than glass lenses, but are more easily scratched, even when scratch resistant coatings are applied. CR-39® lenses tint easily and uniformly, even for those requiring a great deal of refractive correction, but do not hold tints as well as glass. CR-39® plastic can be bleached and re-tinted if fading becomes excessive at some point.

High-index materials (i.e., index of refraction—1.60) are available in both glass and plastic for those who require a large degree of refractive correction and/or desire lighter, thinner lenses. High-index materials are not as widely available, require AR coats to improve optical clarity, and a scratch-resistant coating for durability. In addition, most high-index materials do not accept tints as easily and are less shatter-resistant than polycarbonate.

Coatings

Special coatings can be applied to lens materials for reasons such as those previously mentioned. Crown glass and most plastic lenses require a specific coating to block residual ultraviolet radiation. Plastic and polycarbonate lenses require a scratch-resistant coating to prolong their useful life. The scratch-resistant coating applied to polycarbonate lenses absorbs tints and dyes. High-index materials benefit from AR coatings to improve transmissivity due to their high reflective properties. While AR coats can improve optical clarity, they are extremely porous, attracting water and oils, making the lenses difficult to clean. Lenses with AR coatings should be "sealed" with a smudge- and water-repellant coat that extends the useful life of the AR coat and makes the lenses easier to keep clean. Coatings must be applied correctly, and lenses must be meticulously cleaned for the process to be successful. Coated lenses should be handled with care and not subjected to excessive heat to avoid delamination or crazing.

Tints

The choice of tints for sunglasses is practically infinite. The three most common tints are gray, gray-green, and brown, any of which would be an excellent choice for the aviator. Gray (neutral density filter) is recommended because it distorts color the least. Some pilots, however, report that gray-green and brown tints enhance vividness and minimize scat-

Material Properties	Crown Glass	CR-39 Plastic	Polycarbonate
Index of Refraction Higher number = thinner lens	1.523	1.498	1.586
Specific Gravity Higher number = heavier lens	2.5	1.32	1.20
Dispersion (Abbe value) Higher number = Fewer aberrations	59	58	31
Strength	Temperable	Strong, SRC required	Strongest, SRC applied to lens blank
Characteristics	Coatable, easily fabricated, readily available	Tintable, coatable, easily fabricated, readily available	Coatable, special fabrication equipment required, recommended for children and athletes

Figure 11.3 Properties of the three most common lens materials.

tered (blue and violet) light, thus enhancing contrast in hazy conditions. Yellow, amber, and orange (i.e., "Blue Blockers") tints eliminate short-wavelength light from reaching the wearer's eyes and reportedly sharpen vision, although no scientific studies support this claim.[3] In addition, these tints are known to distort colors, making it difficult to distinguish the color of navigation lights, signals, or color-coded maps and instrument displays. For flying, sunglass lenses should screen out only 70–85% of visible light and not appreciably distort color. Tints that block more than 85% of visible light are not recommended for flying due to the possibility of reduced visual acuity, resulting in difficulty seeing instruments and written material inside the cockpit.

Polarization

Polarized lenses are not recommended for use in the aviation environment. While useful for blocking reflected light from horizontal surfaces such as water or snow, polarization can reduce or eliminate the visibility of instruments that incorporate anti-glare filters. Polarized lenses may also interfere with visibility through an aircraft windscreen by enhancing striations in laminated materials and mask the sparkle of light that reflects off shiny surfaces such as another aircraft's wing or windscreen, which can reduce the time a pilot has to react in a "see-and-avoid" traffic situation.

Photochromic

Glass photochromic lenses (PhotoGray® and PhotoBrown®), like their plastic counterparts (Transitions®), automatically darken when exposed to ultraviolet and become lighter in dim light. Most of the darkening takes place in the first 60 seconds, while lightening may take several minutes. Although most photochromic lenses can get as dark as regular sunglasses, i.e., 20% light transmittance in direct sunlight, warm temperatures (>70°F) can seriously limit their ability to darken and reduced ultraviolet exposure in a cockpit can further limit their effectiveness. In addition, the faded state of photochromic glass lenses may not be clear enough to be useful when flying in cloud cover or at night.

Frames

The selection of sunglass frames is probably more a matter of personal preference than lens material or tint. The frames of an aviator's sunglasses, however, must be functional and not interfere with communication headsets or protective breathing equipment. Frame styles that incorporate small lenses may not be practical, since they allow too much visible light and ultraviolet radiation to pass around the edges of the frame. A sunglass frame should be sturdy enough to take some abuse without breaking, yet light enough to be comfortable. An aviator's sunglasses should fit well so that sudden head movements from turbulence or aerobatic maneuvers do not displace them. Finally, use of a strap is recommended to prevent prescription sunglasses from being accidentally dislodged, or a necklace chain can be used to allow them to be briefly removed and subsequently replaced.

Summary

While adding to the mystique of an aviator, sunglasses protect a pilot's eyes from glare associated with bright sunlight and the harmful effects from exposure to solar radiation.

Lenses for sunglasses that incorporate 100% ultraviolet protection are available in glass, plastic, and polycarbonate materials. Glass and CR-39® plastic lenses have superior optical qualities, while polycarbonate lenses are lighter and more impact-resistant.

The choice of tints for use in the aviation environment should be limited to those that optimize visual performance while minimizing color distortion, such as a neutral gray tint with 15 to 30% light transmittance.

Polarized sunglasses are not recommended because of their possible interaction with displays or other materials in the cockpit environment.

Since sunglasses are an important asset, whether or not refractive correction is required, careful consideration should be used when selecting an appropriate pair for flying.

The technology associated with ophthalmic lenses is continually evolving, with the introduction of new materials, designs, and manufacturing techniques.

Aviators should consult with their eyecare practitioner for the most effective alternatives currently available when choosing a new pair of sunglasses.

References

1. La Commission Internationale de l'Eclairage (CIE). Figures correspond broadly to the effects of UVR on biological tissue.

2. World Meteorological Organization. *Scientific Assessment of Ozone Depletion: 1994*, WMO Global Ozone Research and Monitoring Project–Report No. 37, Geneva, Switzerland: 1995.

3. Rash CE, Manning SD. "For Pilots, Sunglasses are Essential in Vision Protection," *Flight Safety Foundation Human Factors & Aviation Medicine*, July-August 2002; 49(4): 1-8.

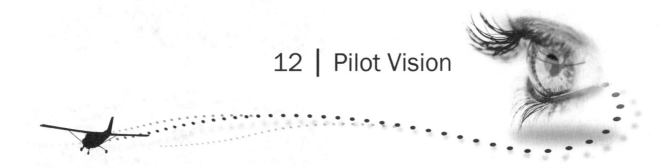

12 | Pilot Vision

Vision is a pilot's most important sense to obtain reference information during flight. Most pilots are familiar with the optical aspects of the eye. Before we start flying, we know whether we have normal uncorrected vision, whether we are farsighted or nearsighted, or have other visual problems. Most of us who have prescription lenses—contacts or eyeglasses—have learned to carry an extra set of glasses with us when we fly, just as a backup. But, vision in flight is far more than a lesson in optics. Seeing involves the transmission of light energy (images) from the exterior surface of the cornea to the interior surface of the retina (inside the eye) and the transference of these signals to the brain.

The Anatomy of the Eye

- Light from an object enters the eye through the cornea and then continues through the pupil.

- The opening (dilation) and closing (constriction) of the pupil is controlled by the iris, which is the colored part of the eye. The function of the pupil is similar to that of the diaphragm of a photographic camera: to control the amount of light.

- The lens is located behind the pupil and its function is to focus light on the surface of the retina.

- The retina is the inner layer of the eyeball that contains photosensitive cells called rods and cones. The function of the retina is similar to

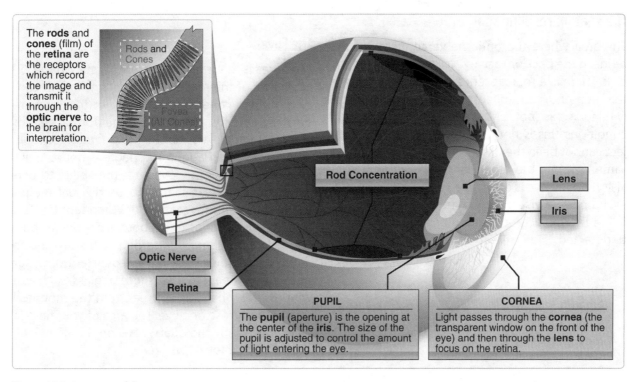

Figure 12.1 Anatomy of the eye.

that of the film in a photographic camera: to record an image.

- The cones are located in higher concentrations than rods in the central area of the retina known as the macula, which measures about 4.5 mm in diameter. The exact center of the macula has a very small depression called the fovea that contains cones only. The cones are used for day or high-intensity light vision. They are involved with central vision to detect detail, perceive color, and identify far-away objects.

- The rods are located mainly in the periphery of the retina—an area that is about 10,000 times more sensitive to light than the fovea. Rods are used for low-light intensity or night vision and are involved with peripheral vision to detect position references including objects (fixed and moving) in shades of grey, but cannot be used to detect detail or to perceive color.

- Light energy (an image) enters the eyes and is transformed by the cones and rods into electrical signals that are carried by the optic nerve to the posterior area of the brain (occipital lobes). This part of the brain interprets the electrical signals and creates a mental image of the actual object that was seen by the person. [Figure 12.1]

The Anatomical Blind Spot

The area where the optic nerve connects to the retina in the back of each eye is known as the optic disk. There is a total absence of cones and rods in this area, and, consequently, each eye is completely blind in this spot. Under normal binocular vision conditions this is not a problem, because an object cannot be in the blind spot of both eyes at the same time. On the other hand, where the field of vision of one eye is obstructed by an object (windshield post), a visual target (another aircraft) could fall in the blind spot of the other eye and remain undetected. [Figure 12.2]

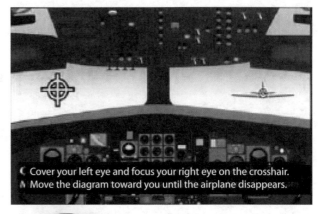

C Cover your left eye and focus your right eye on the crosshair.
N Move the diagram toward you until the airplane disappears.

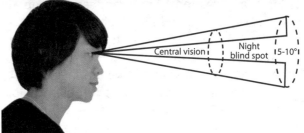

Figure 12.2 Blind spots.

The "Night Blind Spot" appears under conditions of low ambient illumination due to the absence of rods in the fovea, and involves an area 5 to 10 degrees wide in the center of the visual field. Therefore, if an object is viewed directly at night, it may go undetected or it may fade away after initial detection due to the night blind spot.

The Fovea

The fovea is the small depression located in the exact center of the macula that contains a high concentration of cones but no rods, and this is where our vision is most sharp. While the normal field of vision for each eye is about 135 degrees vertically [Figure 12.3] and about 160 degrees horizontally, [Figure 12.4] only the fovea has the ability to perceive and send clear, sharply focused visual images to the brain. This foveal field of vision represents a small conical area of only about 1 degree. To fully appreciate how small a one-degree field is, and to demonstrate foveal field, take a quarter from your pocket and tape it to a flat piece of glass, such as a window. Now back off 4½ feet from the mounted quarter and close one eye. The area of your field of view covered by the quarter is a one-degree field, similar to your foveal vision.

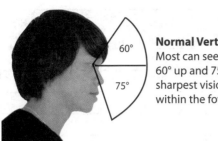

Normal Vertical Vision Field:
Most can see a 135° field —
60° up and 75° down. The
sharpest vision, about 1° is
within the foveal field.

Figure 12.3 Normal vertical vision field.

Now we know that you can see a lot more than just that one-degree cone. But, do you know how little detail you see outside of that foveal cone? For example, outside of a ten-degree cone, concentric to the foveal one-degree cone, you see only about one-tenth of what you can see within the foveal field. In terms of an oncoming aircraft, if you are capable of seeing an aircraft within your foveal field at 5,000 feet away, with peripheral vision you would detect it at 500 feet.

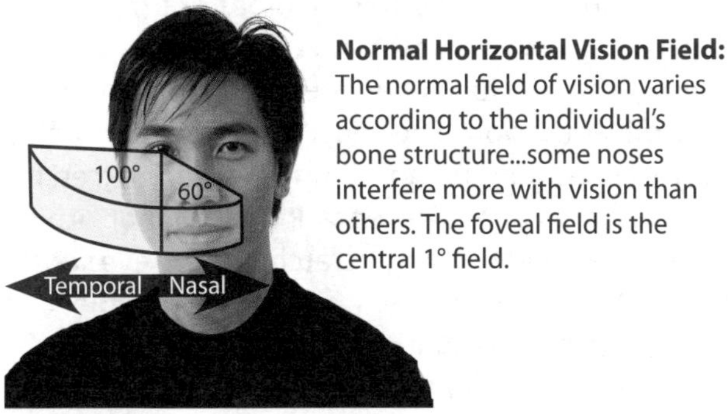

Normal Horizontal Vision Field:
The normal field of vision varies according to the individual's bone structure...some noses interfere more with vision than others. The foveal field is the central 1° field.

Figure 12.4 Normal horizontal vision field.

Another example: using foveal vision we can clearly identify an aircraft flying at a distance of 7 miles; however, using peripheral vision (outside the foveal field) we would require a closer distance of .7 of a mile to recognize the same aircraft. That is why when you were learning to fly, your instructor always told you to "put your head on a swivel," to keep your eyes scanning the wide expanse of space in front of your aircraft.

Types of Vision

Photopic Vision. During daytime or high intensity artificial illumination conditions, the eyes rely on central vision (foveal cones) to perceive and interpret sharp images and color of objects. [Figure 12.5]

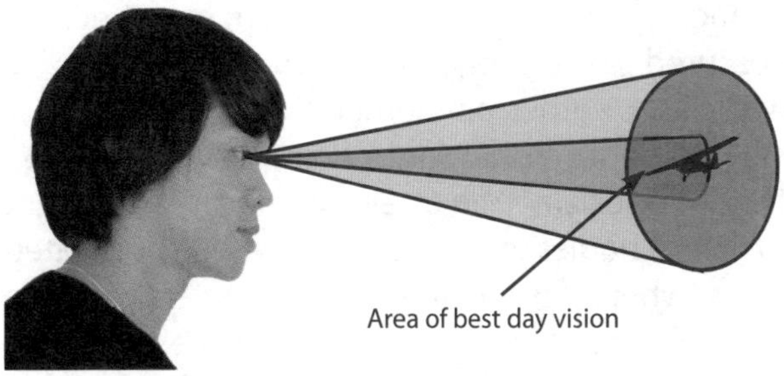

Figure 12.5 Area of best day vision.

Area of best day vision

Mesopic Vision. Occurs at dawn, dusk, or under full moonlight levels, and is characterized by decreasing visual acuity and color vision. Under these conditions, a combination of central (foveal cones) and peripheral (rods) vision is required to maintain appropriate visual performance.

Scotopic Vision. During nighttime, partial moonlight, or low intensity artificial illumination conditions, central vision (foveal cones) becomes ineffective to maintain visual acuity and color perception. Under these conditions, if you look directly at an object for more than a few seconds, the image of the object fades away completely (night blind spot). Peripheral vision (off-center scanning) provides the only means of seeing very dim objects in the dark. [Figure 12.6]

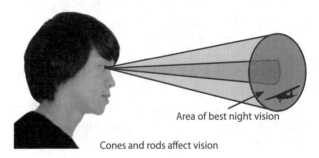

Area of best night vision

Cones and rods affect vision

Figure 12.6 Area of best night vision.

Factors Affecting Vision

The greater the object size, ambient illumination, contrast, viewing time, and atmospheric clarity, the better the visibility of such an object.

During the day, objects can be identified easier at a great distance with good detail resolution. At night, the identification range of dim objects is limited and the detail resolution is poor.

Surface references or the horizon may become obscured by smoke, fog, smog, haze, dust, ice particles, or other phenomena, although visibility may be above Visual Flight Rule (VFR) minimums. This is especially true at airports located adjacent to large bodies of water or sparsely populated areas where few, if any, surface references are available. Lack of horizon or surface reference is common on over-water flights, at night, and in low-visibility conditions.

Excessive ambient illumination, especially from light reflected off the canopy, surfaces inside the aircraft, clouds, water, snow, and desert terrain can produce glare that may cause uncomfortable squinting, eye tearing, and even temporary blindness.

Presence of uncorrected refractive eye disorders such as myopia (nearsightednes—impaired focusing of distant objects), hyperopia (farsightedness—impaired focusing of near objects), astigmatism (impaired focusing of objects in different meridians), or presbyopia (age-related impaired focusing of near objects).

Self-imposed stresses such as self-medication, alcohol consumption (including hangover effects), tobacco use (including withdrawal), hypoglycemia, and sleep deprivation/fatigue can seriously impair your vision. [Figure 12.7]

Inflight exposure to low barometric pressure without the use of supplemental oxygen (above 10,000 ft during the day and above 5,000 feet at night) can result in hypoxia, which impairs visual performance.

Other factors that may have an adverse effect on visual performance include: windscreen haze, improper illumination of the cockpit and/or instruments, scratched and/or dirty instrumentation, use of cockpit red lighting, inadequate cockpit environmental control (temperature and humidity), inappropriate sunglasses and/or prescription glasses/contact lenses, and sustained visual workload during flight.

Altitude (ft)	Smokers (% Reduction)	Non-Smokers (% Reduction)
4,000	20	0
6,000	25	5
10,000	40	20
14,000	55	35
16,000	60	40

Figure 12.7 Comparison of the reduction in night vision at varying altitudes between non-smokers and smokers (8–10% carbon monoxide blood content).

Focusing

The natural ability to focus your eyes is critical to flight safety. It is important to know that normal eyes may require several seconds to refocus when switching views between near (reading charts), intermediate (monitoring instruments), and distant objects (looking for traffic or external visual references). Fatigue can lead to impaired visual focusing, which causes the eyes to overshoot or undershoot the target, and can also affect a pilot's ability to quickly change focus between near, intermediate, and distant vision. The most common symptoms of visual fatigue include blurred vision, excessive tearing, "heavy" eyelid sensation, frontal or orbital headaches, and burning, scratchy, or dry eye sensations. Distance focus, without a specific object to look at, tends to diminish rather quickly. If you fly over water or under hazy conditions with the horizon obscured or between cloud layers at night, your distance focus relaxes after about 60–80 seconds.

If there is nothing specific on which to focus, your eyes revert to a relaxed intermediate focal distance (10 to 30 feet). This means that you are looking without actually seeing anything, which is dangerous. The answer to this phenomenon is to condition your eyes for distant vision. Focus on the most distant object that you can see, even if it's just a wing tip. Do this before you begin scanning the sky in front of you. As you scan, make sure you repeat this re-focusing exercise often.

Dark Adaptation or Night Vision Adaptation

Dark adaptation is the process by which the eyes adapt for optimal night visual acuity under conditions of low ambient illumination. The eyes require about 30 to 45 minutes to fully adapt to minimal lighting conditions. The lower the starting level of illumination, the more rapidly complete dark adaptation is achieved. To minimize the time necessary to achieve complete dark adaptation and to maintain it, you should:

- avoid inhaling carbon monoxide from smoking or exhaust fumes
- get enough Vitamin A in your diet
- adjust instrument and cockpit lighting to the lowest level possible
- avoid prolonged exposure to bright lights
- use supplemental oxygen when flying at night above 5,000 feet (MSL)

If dark-adapted eyes are exposed to a bright light source (searchlights, landing lights, flares, etc.) for a period in excess of 1 second, night vision is temporarily impaired. Exposure to aircraft anti-collision lights does not impair night vision adaptation because the intermittent flashes have a very short duration (less than 1 second).

Visual Scanning

Scanning the sky for other aircraft is a very important factor in avoiding midair collisions, and it should cover all areas of the sky visible from the cockpit. Most of us are instinctively alert for potential head-on encounters with another aircraft. Actually, a study of 50 midair collisions revealed that only 8% were head-on. However, 42% were collisions between aircraft heading in the same direction. So, compared with opposite-direction traffic, your chances of having a midair are over 5 times greater with an aircraft you are overtaking or one that is overtaking you. It is necessary for you to develop and practice a technique that allows the efficient scanning of the surrounding airspace and the monitoring of cockpit instrumentation as well. You can accomplish this by performing a series of short, regularly spaced eye movements that bring successive areas of the sky into the central (foveal) visual field. To scan effectively, scan from right to left or left to right. Begin scanning at the top of the visual field in front of you and then move your eyes inward toward the bottom. Use a stop-turn-stop type eye motion. The duration of each stop should be at least 1 second but not longer than 2 to 3 seconds.

To see and identify objects under conditions of low ambient illumination, avoid looking directly at an object for more than 2 to 3 seconds (because it will bleach out). Instead, use the off-center viewing that consists of searching movements of the eyes (10 degrees above, below, or to either side) to locate an object, and small eye movements to keep the object in sight. By switching your eyes from one off-center point to another every 2 to 3 seconds, you will continue to detect the object in the peripheral field of vision. The reason for using off-center viewing has to do with the location of rods in the periphery of the retina for night or low-intensity night vision (peripheral), and their absence in the center of the retina (fovea). Pilots should practice this off-center scanning technique to improve safety during night flights. [Figure 12.8]

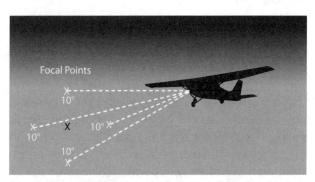

Once a target is detected in the peripheral field of dark–adapted vision, continued surveillance is maintained by use of "off-center" vision, looking 10 degrees right or left and above and below the target, viewing no longer than 2 to 3 seconds at each position.

Figure 12.8 Off-center scanning technique.

A Word about Monocular Vision

A pilot with one eye (monocular), or with effective visual acuity equivalent to monocular (i.e. best corrected distant visual acuity in the poorer eye is no better than 20/200), may be considered for medical certification, any class, through the special issuance procedures of Part 67 (14 CFR 67.401) if:

- A 6-month period has elapsed to allow for adaptation to monocularity; during the adaptation period to monovision, an individual may experience hazy vision and occasional loss of balance.

- A complete evaluation by an eye specialist, as reported on FAA Form 8500-7, Report of Eye Evaluation, reveals no pathology of either eye that could affect the stability of the findings.

- Uncorrected distant visual acuity in the better eye is 20/200 or better and is corrected to 20/20 or better by lenses of no greater power than ±3.5 diopters spherical equivalent.

- The applicant passes an FAA medical flight test.

A Word about Contact Lenses

Use of contact lenses has been permitted to satisfy the distant visual acuity requirements for a civil airman medical certificate since 1976. However, **monovision contact lenses, a technique of fitting older patients who require reading glasses with one contact lens for distant vision and the other lens for near vision, ARE NOT ACCEPTABLE for piloting an aircraft.**

The use of a contact lens in one eye for distant visual acuity and a lens in the other eye for near visual acuity is not acceptable because this procedure makes the pilot alternate his/her vision; that is, a person uses one eye at a time, suppressing the other, and consequently impairs binocular vision and depth perception. Since this is not a permanent condition for either eye in such persons, there is no adaptation, such as occurs with permanent monocularity. Monovision lenses, therefore, should NOT be used by pilots while flying an aircraft.

The Eyes Have It

As a pilot, you are responsible to make sure your vision is equal to the task of flying—that you have good near, intermediate, and distant visual acuity because:

- Distant vision is required for VFR operations including take-off, attitude control, navigation, and landing

- Distant vision is especially important in avoiding midair collisions

- Near vision is required for checking charts, maps, frequency settings, etc.

- Near and intermediate vision are required for checking aircraft instruments

Learn about your own visual strengths and weaknesses. Changes in vision may occur imperceptibly or very rapidly. Periodically self-check your range of visual acuity by trying to see details at near, intermediate, and distant points. If you notice any change in your visual capabilities, bring it to the attention of your Aviation Medical Examiner (AME). And, if you use corrective glasses or contacts, carry an extra pair with you when you fly. Always remember: Vision is a pilot's most important sense.

Key Points

- The sharpest distant focus is only within a one-degree cone.

- Outside of a 10° cone, visual acuity drops 90%.

- Scan the entire horizon, not just the sky in front of your aircraft.

- You are 5 times more likely to have a midair collision with an aircraft flying in the same direction than with one flying in the opposite direction.

- Avoid self-imposed stresses such as self-medication, alcohol consumption, smoking, hypoglycemia, sleep deprivation, and fatigue.

- Do not use monovision contact lenses while you are flying an aircraft.

- Use supplemental oxygen during night flights above 5,000 feet MSL.

- Any pilot can experience visual illusions. Always rely on your instruments to confirm your visual perceptions during flight.

13 | Information for Pilots Considering Laser Eye Surgery

Currently, about 55% of the civilian pilots in the United States must use some form of refractive correction to meet the vision requirements for medical certification. While spectacles are the most common choice for aviators, recent studies show a growing number of pilots have opted for refractive surgical procedures, which include laser refractive surgery. The information in this section describes the benefits as well as possible pitfalls laser refractive surgery offers to those considering these procedures.

What is Refractive Error?

Refractive error prevents light rays from being brought to a single focus on the retina resulting in reduced visual acuity. To see clearly, refractive errors are most often corrected with ophthalmic lenses (glasses, contact lenses). The three principal types of refractive conditions are myopia, hyperopia, and astigmatism. Another ophthalmic condition that also results in blurred near vision is called presbyopia. Presbyopia is a progressive loss of accommodation (decreased ability to focus at near distance due to physiological changes in the eye's crystalline lens) that normally occurs around 40 years of age. Bifocals or reading glasses are necessary to correct this condition.

Myopia (nearsightedness, distant objects appear fuzzy) is a condition in which light rays are focused in front of the retina. About 30% of Americans are myopic.

Hyperopia (farsightedness, near objects appear fuzzy) is a condition in which light rays are focused behind the retina. An estimated 40% of Americans are hyperopic. However, this number may not be accurate. Young hyperopes (<40 years), who can compensate for their farsightedness with their ability to accommodate, are often not counted in this number and some studies incorrectly include presbyopes, who also require plus power lenses to see clearly.

Astigmatism is a condition often caused from an irregular curvature of the cornea. As a result, light is not focused to a single image on the retina. Astigmatism can cause blurred vision at any distance and may occur in addition to myopic or hyperopic conditions. Approximately 60% of the population has some astigmatism.

What is Laser Refractive Surgery?

In October 1995, the Food and Drug Administration (FDA) approved the use of the excimer laser to perform a refractive procedure called Photorefractive Keratectomy (PRK). PRK improves visual acuity by altering the curvature of the cornea through a series of laser pulses. The laser photoablates (vaporizes) the corneal tissue to a predetermined depth and diameter. PRK can be used to correct myopia, hyperopia, and astigmatism. Reported PRK problems such as postoperative pain, prolonged healing period, increased risk of infection, and glare (halos) at night, has resulted in Laser in situ Keratomileusis (LASIK) becoming the preferred choice for refractive surgery by patients and eyecare practitioners. A survey in the United States found that the percentage of refractive surgeons performing PRK had decreased from 26% in 1997 to less than 1% in 2002.

LASIK is performed using two FDA approved devices: the microkeratome and excimer laser. During the LASIK procedure, the microkeratome slices a thin flap from the top of the cornea, leaving it connected by a small hinge of tissue. The corneal flap is folded aside and the excimer laser is used to reshape the underlying corneal stroma. The flap is then returned to its original position. [Figure 13.1]

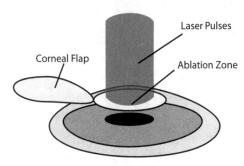

Figure 13.1 LASIK procedure.

Is LASIK an Option for Me?

An eye care specialist should thoroughly evaluate your current ocular health and correction requirements to determine whether you are a suitable candidate for refractive surgery. Clinical trials have established the following selection criteria for LASIK.

Selection Criteria

- Age 18 years or older
- Stable refractive error (less than .50 diopters [D] change within the last year) correctable to 20/40 or better
- Less than -15.00 D of myopia and up to 6 to 7 D of astigmatism
- Less than +6.00 D of hyperopia and less than 6 D of astigmatism
- No gender restriction, with the exception of pregnancy
- Pupil size less than or equal to 6 mm (in normal room lighting)
- Realistic expectations of final results (with a complete understanding of the benefits, as well as the possible risks)

In addition to conforming to the above criteria, it is important that you possess normal ocular health and be free of pre-existing conditions that may contraindicate LASIK.

Contraindications

- Collagen vascular disease (corneal ulceration or melting)
- Ocular disease (dry eye, keratoconus, glaucoma, incipient cataracts, herpes simplex keratitis, corneal edema)
- Systemic disorders (diabetes, rheumatoid arthritis, lupus, HIV, AIDS)
- History of side effects from steroids
- Signs of keratoconus
- Use of some acne medication (e.g., Accutane and/or Cordarone)

Is LASIK Safe for Pilots?

Aviators considering LASIK should know that in initial FDA trials reporting high success rates (≥90%) and low complication rates (<1%), the criteria for success varied. In most clinical studies, success was defined as 20/40 or better distant uncorrected visual acuity (UCVA) under normal room lighting with high contrast targets, not 20/20 or better UCVA. While the majority of patients do experience dramatic improvement in vision after laser refractive surgery, there is no guarantee that perfect UCVA will be the final outcome. Even successful procedures may leave many patients with a small amount of residual refractive error that requires an ophthalmic device (eyeglasses or contact lenses) to obtain 20/20 visual acuity. If overcorrection results, patients may need reading glasses.

Compared to its predecessor (PRK), LASIK requires higher technical skill by the surgeon because a corneal flap must be created. Although rare, loss of best corrected visual acuity (BCVA) can occur when there are surgical complications such as those summarized below.

Surgical Complications

- Decentered or detached corneal flap
- Decentered ablation zone
- Button-hole flap (flap cut too thin resulting in a hole)
- Perforation of the eye

Operation of an aircraft is a visually demanding activity performed in an environment that is not always user friendly. This becomes particularly evident if the choice of vision correction is ill-suited for the task. While the risk of serious vision-threatening complications after having LASIK is low (<1%), some complications could have a significant impact on visual performance in a cockpit environment.

Relative Risk of Post-Surgical Complications

- Prolonged healing periods: 3 months or more
- Night glare (halos, starbursts): 1 in 50
- Under/over-correction: less than 1 in 100
- Increased intraocular pressure: non significant
- Corneal haze: 1 in 1,000
- Corneal scarring: non significant
- Loss of BCVA: 1 in 100
- Infection: 1 in 5,000
- Corneal flap complications (dislocated flap, epithelial ingrowth): less than 1 in 100

Following LASIK, patients are cautioned to avoid rubbing their eyes and to stay out of swimming pools, hot tubs, or whirlpools for at least a week. Contact sports should be avoided for a minimum of 2 weeks, and many eye surgeons recommend wearing safety eyewear while playing sports. Even after the patient's vision has stabilized and healing appears complete, the corneal flap may not be completely re-adhered. There have been reports of corneal flap displacement due to trauma up to 38 months after the procedure.

After surgery, patients are cautioned to not wear eye makeup or use lotions and creams around their eyes for a minimum of 2 weeks and to discard all previously used makeup to reduce the risk of infection.

In some instances, LASIK may be an option for patients with higher refractive error than can be safely corrected with PRK or those with conditions that can delay healing (e.g., lupus, rheumatoid arthritis). Since LASIK minimizes the area of the epithelium surgically altered, it reduces some of the risks associated with delayed healing. Additionally, ablation of the underlying stromal tissue results in less cor-neal haze and the tendency for the cornea to revert back to the original refractive condition during the healing process (refractive regression), which improves predictability. Most patients do not require long-term, postoperative steroid use, decreasing the possibility of steroid-induced complications (cataract, glaucoma).

As with any invasive procedure, there are surgical risks, and the recovery process often varies with each individual. Post-LASIK patients report experiencing mild irritation, sensitivity to bright light, and tearing for a few days after surgery. For most, vision stabilizes within 3 months to near-predicted results, and residual night glare usually diminishes within 6 months. In rare cases, symptoms have lingered longer than a year. Earlier versions of LASIK used a smaller ablation zone which sometimes resulted in glare problems at night. Ablation zones have an area of transition between treated and untreated corneal tissue. As the pupil dilates and becomes larger than the ablation zone, light (car headlights, streetlights, and traffic signal lights) entering through these transition areas becomes distorted, resulting in aberrations perceived as glare. These patients often complain of difficulties seeing under low-light conditions.

Patients that develop postoperative haze during the healing process have complained of glare (halos and starbursts). Furthermore, it has been reported that exposure to ultraviolet radiation or bright sunlight may result in refractive regression and late-onset corneal haze. It is therefore recommended that all refractive surgery patients wear sunglasses with UV protection and to refrain from using tanning beds for several months after surgery.

For those with larger amounts of refractive correction, the predictability of the resulting refractive correction is less exact. This can lead to under-correction (requiring an additional laser enhancement procedure and/or corrective lenses) or over-correction of the refractive error. In the case of overcorrection, premature presbyopia and the need for reading glasses can result.

It has been reported that there can be a slower recovery of BCVA and UCVA with hyperopic LASIK compared with those having myopic LASIK. This is especially true for older patients who may be even less likely to achieve UCVA of 20/20 or better. (Note: Loss of BCVA is reportedly 5 to 15 times more likely with refractive surgery than from the use of extended-wear contact lenses.)

Older patients with presbyopia may opt for monovision LASIK, which corrects the dominant eye for distant vision and the other eye for near vision. The procedure is intended to eliminate the need for a patient to wear corrective lenses for near and distant vision. Anisometropia (difference in correction between the eyes) induced by monovision may result in decreased binocular vision, contrast sensitivity, and stereo acuity. After an adaptation period, patients are often able to see and function normally. Patients who report blurred vision, difficulty with night driving, and other visual tasks in low-light conditions typically do not adapt to monovision and may require an enhancement on their non-dominant eye so that both eyes are fully corrected for distant vision. Airmen who seek monovision correction should consult an eye care practitioner to assist them in compliance with standards outlined in the "Guide for Aviation Medical Examiners" (see below):

> Airmen who opt for monovision LASIK must initially wear correction (i.e., glasses or contact lens) for near vision eye while operating an aircraft. After a 6-month period of adaptation, they may apply for a Statement of Demonstrated Ability (SODA) with a medical flight test. If the airman is successful, the lens requirement is removed from their medical certificate.

Advances in Refractive Surgery

Wavefront LASIK

Eye care specialists have traditionally used standard measurement techniques that identify and correct lower-order aberrations, such as nearsightedness, farsightedness, and astigmatism. However, no two people share the same eye irregularities or have similar refractive needs. Vision is unique and as personal as fingerprints or DNA.

Wavefront technology allows eye surgeons to customize the LASIK procedure for each eye, providing the possibility of even better vision. The FDA approved the first system for general use in October 2002. A laser beam is sent through the eye to the retina and is reflected back through the pupil, measuring the irregularities of the light wave (wavefront) as it emerges from the eye. This process produces a three-dimensional map of the eye's optical system. Measuring the cornea's imperfections or aberrations in this way allows the refractive surgeon to develop a personalized treatment plan for the patient's unique vision needs. Correcting the patient's specific imperfections can result in sharper vision, better contrast sensitivity, and reduces problems associated with higher-order aberrations after surgery, such as haloes and blurred images. Studies indicate that 90–94% of patients receiving wavefront LASIK achieved visual acuity of 20/20 or better. However, those with thin corneas, high degrees of aberrations, severe dry eyes, or conditions affecting the lens and vitreous fluid inside the eye may not be good candidates for wavefront LASIK.

Other Advances in Refractive Surgery

The eye's optical system creates a limit as to how wide and deep the laser ablation should be, i.e., the wider the ablation, the deeper the laser must ablate into the cornea, which may result in delayed healing and prolonged visual recovery. The development of new lasers allows the creation of a wider ablation zone while removing the least amount of tissue. Studies have shown that this reduces problems with night vision and other side effects associated with laser refractive surgery.

Laser technology that provides variable optical zone sizes and beam shapes with scanning capabilities allows the eye surgeon greater flexibility in developing a more personalized laser vision procedure. A spot laser may be adjusted so minimal spherical aberrations are produced and a larger optical zone is created. Results from clinical trials indicate that 67% of eyes had UCVA of 20/16 or better and 25% had 20/12.5 or better. Additionally, there was an overall improvement in nighttime visual function and night driving, which is achieved by preserving the optical zone size and better shaping of the ablation profile.

During traditional LASIK, the corneal flap is created with a mechanical microkeratome manipulated by the surgeon's hand. While this method has worked well over the years, the performance of these devices can be unpredictable and is the source of a majority of surgical complications. These difficulties result in irregularities in thickness between the central and peripheral areas of the flap that can induce postoperative astigmatism.

The IntraLase Femtosecond Laser Keratome, which received FDA approval in December 1999, is the first blade-free technology for creating the corneal flap. The laser keratome beam passes into the cornea at a predetermined depth, producing a precise cut that is reportedly more accurate than the microkeratome. Corneal flaps made with the laser keratome appear to adhere more tightly to the corneal bed at the end of the procedure, which may eliminate problems with long-term flap displacement. A reported disadvantage to this new technology is that surgical time is increased, leaving the stroma exposed several minutes longer, which has led to reported complaints of photophobia and eye irritation for up to two days after surgery. While it may take longer (4 to 7 days) to recover good vision, the approach appears to be associated with a lower incidence of dry eyes, corneal complications, and enhancement procedures compared with traditional LASIK.

The FAA requires that civil airmen with refractive surgical procedures (e.g., PRK, LASIK) discontinue flying until their eyecare specialist has determined that their vision is stable and there are no significant adverse effects or complications. The airman should submit one of two documents to the FAA (a report from their eyecare specialist or "Report of Eye Evaluation" [FAA-8500-7]). These reports can be submitted directly to the Aerospace Medical Certification Division when released from care, or to their Aviation Medical Examiner during their next flight physical. This report should state:

". . . . that the airman meets the visual acuity standards and the report of eye evaluation indicates healing is complete, visual acuity remains stable, and the applicant does not suffer sequela, such as glare intolerance, halos, rings, impaired night vision, or any other complications . . . ." (Guide for Aviation Medical Examiners, July 2005)

If you are a pilot contemplating refractive surgery, consult an eyecare specialist to determine if you are a good candidate for laser refractive surgery. Although the FAA and most major air carriers allow laser refractive surgery, professional aviators should consider how it could affect their occupational and certification status. As with any invasive procedure, there are many variables that can influence the final outcome. You should understand all risks as well as the benefits before electing to have a procedure performed that could compromise your visual performance in the cockpit.

14 | Smoke

Smoke Toxicity

The specter of fire in the air is a pilot's recurrent nightmare...

Fire is an integral part of our everyday life, and smoke is one of its products. There have always been efforts to control fire and use it for constructive purposes, but even then, accidental fires do occur and fire continues to cause loss of lives and property.

Uncontrolled fires threaten homes, factories, and transportation systems. The specter of fire in the air is a pilot's recurrent nightmare, carried over from the early days of fabric covered aircraft, when the time between ignition and loss of the aircraft could be measured in relatively few minutes.

Modern aircraft benefit from flame-retardant materials and improved fire extinguishing systems to such an extent that in-flight fires are rare occurrences.

However, survivable crashes followed by fire happen, primarily from fuel spills around the downed aircraft. In the confined environment of an aircraft cabin, the presence of smoke automatically indicates the existence of an emergency situation.

Extinguishment of fires obviously has first priority, but smoke inhalation should be recognized as a very real danger while this is being accomplished. Inhalation of toxic gases in smoke is the primary cause of fatalities in most fires — this is true whether the fire is in an aircraft cabin, a residential bedroom, or a high-rise building. Smoke gases do not need to reach lethal levels to seriously impair pilot performance. Sublethal exposures can cause even experienced pilots to make potentially fatal mistakes.

In view of the seriousness of any aircraft fire, let us examine the various aspects of fire and smoke.

Fire
Each fire is different...

Fire is a complex, dynamic, physicochemical event and is the result of a rapid chemical reaction generating smoke, heat, flame, and light. Each fire is different. Smoke composition and heat generated in a fire depend on types of burning materials and environmental conditions.

Smoke
Its gases could be toxic...

Smoke is a complex of particulate matter, as well as a variety of invisible combustion gases and vapors suspended in the fire atmosphere. Smoke may diminish light and obscure vision, and its gases could be toxic.

Smoke Gases

Carbon dioxide levels increase and oxygen concentrations decrease...

Carbon monoxide and hydrogen cyanide are the two principal toxic combustion gases. Most cabin furnishings contain carbon and will generate both carbon monoxide and carbon dioxide when burned; carbon monoxide can also be released from faulty cabin heaters. Burning wool, silk, and many nitrogen-containing synthetics will produce the more toxic hydrogen cyanide gas. Irritant gases, such as hydrogen chloride and acrolein, are generated from burning wiring insulation and some other cabin materials. Generally, carbon dioxide levels increase and oxygen concentrations decrease during fires.

Smoke Effects
At high altitude, the effects are greatly enhanced...

Visual smoke can delay escape from a fire, while the irritant gases can induce tears, pain, and disorientation. The visual obscuration is obvious, but the subtle effects of carbon monoxide and hydrogen cyanide inhalation, although less readily detected, can cause physical incapacitation and subsequent death. Toxicologically, carbon monoxide combines with the hemoglobin in blood and interferes with the oxygen supply to tissues, while hydrogen cyanide inhibits oxygen utilization at the cellular level. Carbon dioxide, a relatively innocuous fire gas, increases the respiration rate causing an increase in the uptake of the other combustion gases. The decreased oxygen level found in most fire scenarios further enhances the problem of getting enough oxygen to the biological sites to maintain normal function. Continued inhalation of these gases can result in severe hypoxia. At high altitude where oxygen levels are lower, the effects of carbon monoxide and hydrogen cyanide are greatly enhanced.

Signs and Symptoms
Not all symptoms will necessarily be experienced...

Carbon monoxide poisoning produces headache, weakness, nausea, dizziness, confusion, dimness of vision, disturbance of judgment, and unconsciousness followed by coma and death. Although carbon monoxide causes deleterious effects on the central nervous system, death usually occurs from cardiotoxicity. Not all symptoms will necessarily be experienced by every individual exposed to this gas. Some have succumbed from inhaling low carbon monoxide levels, while others have survived breathing higher concentrations. Hydrogen cyanide poisoning signs and symptoms are weakness, dizziness, headache, nausea, vomiting, coma, convulsions, and death. Death results from respiratory arrest. Hydrogen cyanide gas acts very rapidly—symptoms and death can both occur quickly.

Survival
Knowledge of the less obvious hazards and a few simple preparations can increase one's chances...

There is no universal best procedure to follow in the event of an aircraft fire because no two fires are likely to be the same. Extinguishing the fire, if possible, is the immediate priority. An equally obvious second priority is to breathe as little smoke for as short a duration as possible.

Some larger aircraft are supplied with portable, self-contained breathing masks for the crew, but small private aircraft usually are not. Any cloth held over the nose and mouth will provide protection from smoke particulates; if the cloth is wet, it will also absorb most of the water-soluble gases (i.e., hydrogen cyanide and hydrogen chloride).

Cabin venting will reduce the concentrations of combustion gases, but is not usually a viable option while actually fighting the fire. Knowledge of the less obvious hazards and a few simple preparations can increase one's chances for survival in an aircraft fire. A small, hand-held fire extinguisher can be used to put out small onboard fires. Careful inspection and maintenance of cabin heaters will minimize the chance of carbon monoxide leakage into the cabin air system. A carbon monoxide detector could also be installed in the cockpit to detect the presence of this colorless, odorless gas. As always, planning your probable actions before an emergency arises will increase your chances for acting quickly and correctly.

Remember...

- Fires are the main hazard for the occupants of a survivable crash
- A fire generates smoke, heat, flame, and light
- Inhalation of toxic gases in smoke is the primary cause of death in most fires
- Carbon monoxide and hydrogen cyanide are the main toxic gases in smoke
- Exposure to carbon monoxide can also be the result of faulty heaters
- A wet cloth held over the nose and mouth provides some protection from smoke inhalation
- A small, hand-held fire extinguisher should always be carried aboard general aviation aircraft
- Install a carbon monoxide detector in the cockpit

15 | Carbon Monoxide: A Deadly Menace

An "Unconscious" Landing

Plane Lands Itself in Hayfield as Pilot Slumbers

Physician Robert Frayser had lifted off in his Comanche 400 from the North Bend, Kansas, airport at 7 a.m., en route for a meeting in Topeka. He was flying alone, cruising at 5,500 feet on autopilot, with the sun coming up on a clear, beautiful day. Per established routine, he switched the fuel selector to the auxiliary tank and set up the navigation system for nearby Topeka.

About 90 minutes later, Dr. Frayser found himself in a hay field. The engine was silent. He was confused, disoriented, and groggy as he struggled to rouse himself from a deep sleep. His head was throbbing.

Thinking he was still in the air, he went through his landing checklist. As he became more oriented to his surroundings, a new reality dawned: The airplane's right wing was nearly torn off from an impact with a tree, but the plane was otherwise intact. Aside from a fractured wrist, minor cuts, and bruises, he seemed to be relatively uninjured. But he had no idea where he was. He had no memory of landing.

Dr. Frayser stated that there were no early warnings or symptoms to alert him. "I just went to sleep." The plane, trimmed for cruise flight and on autopilot, flew a perfectly straight course over Kansas and into Missouri until it ran out of fuel, and then the autopilot gently brought the Comanche in for landing.

Since the engine had stopped, no one heard the aircraft glide to a landing on the open field. "I was alone, disoriented, injured, and had a severe headache and ringing in my ears," he said.

Extracting himself from the aircraft, he struggled a quarter of a mile through snow-covered fields for help, finally stumbling onto a farmhouse. Dr. Frayser was taken by ambulance to a hospital, where the emergency room physician put him on 100 percent oxygen to overcome near-fatal blood levels of carboxyhemoglobin.

Carbon monoxide poisoning from a cracked muffler had allowed the deadly, odorless gas to seep into the cabin through the heater and caused him to fall asleep. The crack, which had apparently opened after the last annual inspection, was concealed by the heat shield and could not be detected during the pre-flight inspection. "The crack could have been there for a long time, just waiting for someone to turn on the heater," he said. Frayser did not have a carbon monoxide detector on board to alert him of its presence.

Another 30 minutes in the air might have been fatal. Carbon monoxide poisoning would have claimed another victim.

Overlooked Safety Issue

Carbon monoxide poisoning is a safety issue that pilots tend to ignore, even though it is the most common industrial poisoning accident in the United States. When carbon monoxide poisoning occurs, it can have significant and fatal consequences for aircraft occupants.

Carbon monoxide is a by-product of the incomplete combustion of carbon-containing materials. Aviation fuel contains carbon and is a ready source of carbon monoxide when burned. Expect carbon monoxide whenever an internal combustion engine is operating, and even though piston engines produce the highest concentrations of carbon monoxide, exhaust from turbine engines could also cause carbon monoxide poisoning. In addition, expect carbon monoxide whenever a fire occurs, as commonly happens in a post-crash environment.

Carbon monoxide is truly a hidden menace because by itself, it is both a colorless and odorless gas. An individual would not be aware of its presence until symptoms developed, or during treatment it was determined exposure had occurred. The least desirable situation would be incapacitation. In this case, the victim is powerless to do anything about the exposure. Fortunately, because it is a by-product of combustion, carbon monoxide is frequently associated with other gases that do have an odor and color.

By avoiding an environment with known combustion fumes, you will also avoid carbon monoxide. The true problem comes when exposure is so gradual that you don't perceive it. You can become incapacitated before you can vacate the environment. In an airplane, the result most likely will be a fatal accident.

Why Carbon Monoxide Poisoning Should Concern Pilots

What is not known is the full extent of carbon monoxide poisoning in aviation. Analysis of toxicology samples from fatal U.S. aircraft accidents between 1967 and 1993 showed that at least 360 victims had been exposed to sufficient carbon monoxide before or after the crash to impair their abilities. Non-fatal carbon monoxide poisoning in aviation is likely a more common occurrence than currently believed. No one is sure how many times pilots or passengers became ill, not realizing they had been exposed to carbon monoxide. Because no significant incident or incapacitation occurred, the matter was not reported and, hence, not investigated. Symptoms that could be attributed to airsickness, altitude hypoxia, fatigue, or a variety of other conditions actually could have been carbon monoxide poisoning.

Exposure and symptoms may occur repeatedly over several flights until, finally, someone suspects carbon monoxide or, tragically, an accident claims a victim. No database presently exists that accurately collects or tracks non-fatal aviation carbon monoxide exposure information.

Toxicity Mechanism

Carbon monoxide has a very high affinity for hemoglobin, the molecule in blood responsible for transporting oxygen through the body. Carbon monoxide has affinity of 240 times that of oxygen. Carbon monoxide tightly attaches to the hemoglobin, creating the compound carboxyhemoglobin, which prevents oxygen from binding, thereby blocking its transport. The result is hypoxia but through a mechanism different from that produced by altitude. However, with respect to symptoms, the end-effects can be very similar.

There should be little or no carbon monoxide in the blood of individuals who have not been exposed to smoke or other by-products of combustion. People living in polluted urban environments may have between 3–10% carboxyhemoglobin concentrations because of the carbon monoxide contained in the smoke and fumes they inhale, while a cigar smoker could have up to 15%. People in certain occupations such as foundry workers, welders, mechanics, firefighters, and tollbooth or tunnel attendants that expose them to products of combustion may also have elevated carbon monoxide baseline levels.

Symptoms

The most common symptoms of carbon monoxide exposure are shown in Figure 15.1. These symptoms are typical for an individual with normal hemoglobin at sea level. You can expect these symptoms to worsen at altitude and/or appear sooner than they otherwise would. Wide personal variations may also occur, depending on the circumstances and whether or not the individual smokes.

% of CO in Blood	Typical Symptoms
<10%	None
10-20%	Slight headache
21-30%	Headache, slight increase in respirations, drowsiness
31-40%	Headache, impaired judgment, shortness of breath, increasing drowsiness, blurring of vision
41-50%	Pounding headache, confusion, marked shortness of breath, marked drowsiness, increasing blurred vision
>51%	Unconsciousness, eventual death if victim is not removed from source of CO

Figure 15.1 Carbon monoxide (CO) blood levels and possible symptoms.

Protection from Carbon Monoxide Exposure

First and foremost is pilot education and awareness. Pilots must understand the danger posed by carbon monoxide poisoning and should be alert to the symptoms.

Any unusual cabin smell or sensation of illness should call for immediate troubleshooting:

- Turn the cabin heat fully off.
- Increase the rate of cabin fresh air ventilation to the maximum.
- Open windows if the flight profile and aircraft's operating manual permit such an action.
- If available (provided it does not represent a safety or fire hazard), consider using supplemental oxygen.

- Land as promptly as possible.
- Do not hesitate to let Air Traffic Control know of your concerns, and ask for vectors to the nearest airport.
- Once on the ground, seek medical attention.
- Before continuing the flight, have the aircraft inspected by a certified mechanic.

Safeguards

- The best protection against carbon monoxide poisoning is to avoid exposure.
- Aircraft operators and pilots must ensure that heating/ventilation systems and exhaust manifolds in their aircraft are all in good working order, as specified by the manufacturer and the Federal Aviation Administration.
- Certified mechanics must conduct all required inspections.
- Special attention should be paid to older aircraft because of corrosion or simple wear and tear.
- A certified mechanic should verify firewall and aircraft structural integrity and seal any defects.
- Finally, several devices are available to monitor for carbon monoxide. The least expensive are handheld or stick-on colorimetric devices that change color in the presence of carbon monoxide. While effective, they are not perfect or foolproof. Powered detectors for aviation use are available as either portable or panel-mounted units and provide greater reliability.

16 | Spatial Disorientation: Visual Illusions

Spatial Orientation

Spatial orientation defines our natural ability to maintain our body orientation and/or posture in relation to the surrounding environment (physical space) at rest and during motion. Genetically speaking, humans are designed to maintain spatial orientation on the ground. The flight environment is hostile and unfamiliar to the human body; it creates sensory conflicts and illusions that make spatial orientation difficult, and, in some cases, even impossible to achieve. Statistics show that between 5 to 10% of all general aviation accidents can be attributed to spatial disorientation, and 90% of these accidents are fatal.

Spatial Orientation on the Ground

Good spatial orientation on the ground relies on the effective perception, integration, and interpretation of visual, vestibular (organs of equilibrium located in the inner ear), and proprioceptive (receptors located in the skin, muscles, tendons, and joints) sensory information. Changes in linear acceleration, angular acceleration, and gravity are detected by the vestibular system and the proprioceptive receptors, and then compared in the brain with visual information. [Figure 16.1]

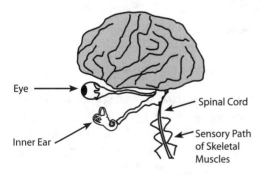

Figure 16.1 Sensory organs transmission paths.

Spatial Orientation In Flight

Spatial orientation in flight is sometimes difficult to achieve because the various types of sensory stimuli (visual, vestibular, and proprioceptive) vary in magnitude, direction, and frequency. Any differences or discrepancies between visual, vestibular, and proprioceptive sensory inputs result in a "sensory mismatch" that can produce illusions and lead to spatial disorientation.

Vision and Spatial Orientation

Visual references provide the most important sensory information to maintain spatial orientation on the ground and during flight, especially when the body and/or the environment are in motion. Even birds, reputable flyers, are unable to maintain spatial orientation and fly safely when deprived of vision (due to clouds or fog). Only bats have developed the ability to fly without vision but have replaced their vision with auditory echolocation. So, it should not be any surprise to us that, when we fly under conditions of limited visibility, we have problems maintaining spatial orientation.

Central Vision

Central vision, also known as foveal vision, is involved with the identification of objects and the perception of colors. During instrument flight rules (IFR) flights, central vision allows pilots to acquire information from the flight instruments that is processed by the brain to provide orientational information. During visual flight rules (VFR) flights, central vision allows pilots to acquire external information (monocular and binocular) to make judgments of distance, speed, and depth.

Peripheral Vision

Peripheral vision, also known as ambient vision, is involved with the perception of movement (self and surrounding environment) and provides peripheral reference cues to maintain spatial orientation. This capability enables orientation independent from central vision and that is why we can walk while reading. With peripheral vision, motion of the surrounding environment produces a perception of self-motion even if we are standing or sitting still.

Visual References

Visual references that provide information about distance, speed, and depth of visualized objects include:

- Comparative size of known objects at different distances.
- Comparative form or shape of known objects at different distances.
- Relative velocity of images moving across the retina. Nearby objects are perceived as moving faster than distant objects.
- Interposition of known objects. One object placed in front of another is perceived as being closer to the observer.
- Varying texture or contrast of known objects at different distances. Object detail and contrast are lost with distance.
- Differences in illumination perspective of objects due to light and shadows.
- Differences in aerial perspective of visualized objects. More distant objects are seen as bluish and blurry.

The flight attitude of an airplane is generally determined by the pilot's visual reference to the natural horizon. When the natural horizon is obscured, attitude can sometimes be maintained by visual reference to the surface below. If neither horizon nor surface visual references exist, the airplane's attitude can only be determined by artificial means such as an attitude indicator or other flight instruments. Surface references or the natural horizon may at times become obscured by smoke, fog, smog, haze, dust, ice particles, or other phenomena, although visibility may be above VFR minimums. This is especially true at airports located adjacent to large bodies of water or sparsely populated areas, where few, if any, surface references are available. Lack of horizon or surface reference is common on over-water flights, at night, or in low visibility conditions.

Visual Illusions

Visual illusions are familiar to most of us. As children, we learned that railroad tracks—contrary to what our eyes showed us—don't come to a point at the horizon. Even under conditions of good visibility, you can experience visual illusions including:

Aerial Perspective Illusions may make you change (increase or decrease) the slope of your final approach. They are caused by runways with different widths, upsloping or downsloping runways, and upsloping or downsloping final approach terrain. Pilots learn to recognize a normal final approach by developing and recalling a mental image of the expected relationship between the length and the width of an average runway. [Figure 16.2]

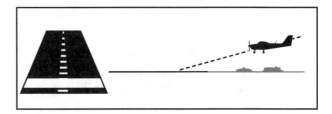

Figure 16.2 Normal final approach.

A final approach over a flat terrain with an upsloping runway may produce the visual illusion of a high-altitude final approach. If you believe this illusion, you may respond by pitching the aircraft nose down to decrease the altitude, which, if performed too close to the ground, may result in an accident [Figure 16.3].

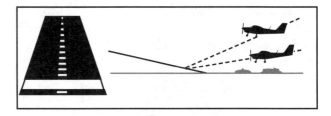

Figure 16.3 Final approach with upsloping runway.

A final approach over a flat terrain with a downsloping runway may produce the visual illusion of a low-altitude final approach. If you believe this illusion, you may respond by pitching the aircraft nose up to increase the altitude, which may result in a low-altitude stall or a missed approach. [Figure 16.4]

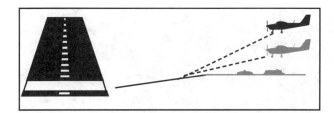

Figure 16.4 Final approach with downsloping runway.

A final approach over an upsloping terrain with a flat runway may produce the visual illusion of a low-altitude final approach. If you believe this illusion, you may respond by pitching the aircraft nose up to increase the altitude, which may result in a low-altitude stall or a missed approach. [Figure 16. 5]

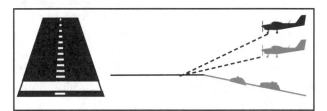

Figure 16.5 Final approach over upsloping terrain with a flat runway.

A final approach over a downsloping terrain with a flat runway may produce the visual illusion of a high-altitude final approach. If you believe this illusion, you may respond by pitching the aircraft nose down to decrease the altitude, which, if performed too close to the ground, may result in an accident. [Figure 16.6]

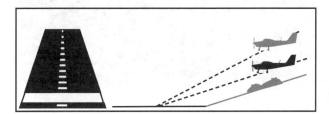

Figure 16.6 Final approach over downsloping terrain with a flat runway.

A final approach to an unusually narrow runway or an unusually long runway may produce the visual illusion of a high-altitude final approach. If you believe this illusion, you may respond by pitching the aircraft nose down to decrease the altitude, which, if performed too close to the ground may result in an accident. [Figure 16.7]

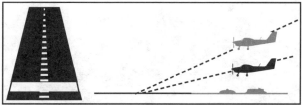

Figure 16.7 Final approach to an unusually long or narrow runway.

A final approach to an unusually wide runway may produce the visual illusion of a low-altitude final approach. If you believe this illusion, you may respond by pitching the aircraft nose up to increase the altitude, which may result in a low-altitude stall or a missed approach. [Figure 16.8]

Figure 16.8 Final approach to an unusually wide runway.

A **Black-Hole Approach Illusion** can happen during a final approach at night (no stars or moonlight) over water or unlighted terrain to a lighted runway beyond which the horizon is not visible. In the example [Figure 16.9], when peripheral visual cues are not available to help you orient yourself relative to the earth, you may have the illusion of being upright and may perceive the runway to be tilted left and upsloping. However, with the horizon visible [Figure 16.10], you can easily orient yourself correctly using your central vision.

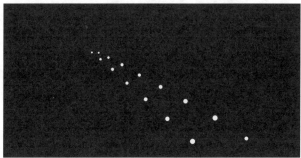

Figure 16.9 Black-hole approach illusion.

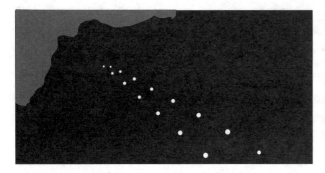

Figure 16.10 Night approach with the horizon visible.

A particularly hazardous black-hole illusion involves approaching a runway under conditions with no lights before the runway and with city lights or rising terrain beyond the runway. These conditions may produce the visual illusion of a high-altitude final approach. If you believe this illusion, you may respond by lowering your approach slope. [Figure 16.11]

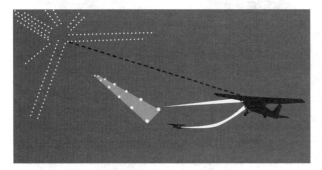

Figure 16.11 Black-hole illusion with city lights or rising terrain beyond the runway.

The **Autokinetic Illusion** gives you the impression that a stationary object is moving in front of the airplane's path; it is caused by staring at a fixed single point of light (ground light or a star) in a totally dark and featureless background. This illusion can cause a misperception that such a light is on a collision course with your aircraft. [Figure 16.12]

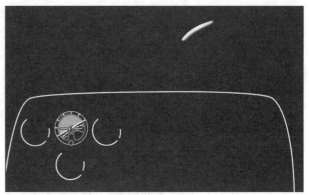

Figure 16.12 Autokinetic illusion.

False Visual Reference Illusions may cause you to orient your aircraft in relation to a false horizon; these illusions are caused by flying over a banked cloud, night flying over featureless terrain with ground lights that are indistinguishable from a dark sky with stars, or night flying over a featureless terrain with a clearly defined pattern of ground lights and a dark, starless sky. [Figure 16.13]

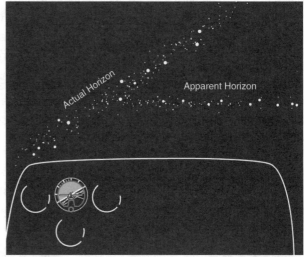

Figure 16.13 False horizon illusion.

Vection Illusion. A common example is when you are stopped at a traffic light in your car and the car next to you edges forward. Your brain interprets this peripheral visual information as though you are moving backwards and makes you apply additional pressure to the brakes. A similar illusion can happen while taxiing an aircraft.

How to Prevent Spatial Disorientation

- Take the opportunity to personally experience sensory illusions in a Barany chair, a Vertigon, a GYRO, or a Virtual Reality Spatial Disorientation Demonstrator (VRSDD). By experiencing sensory illusions first hand (on the ground), pilots are better prepared to recognize a sensory illusion when it happens during flight and to take immediate action. The Aeromedical Education Division of the FAA Civil Aerospace Medical Institute offers spatial disorientation demonstrations with the GYRO and the VRSDD in Oklahoma City and at all of the major airshows in the continental U.S.

- Obtain training and maintain your proficiency in aircraft control by reference to instruments.

- When flying at night or in reduced visibility, use and rely on your flight instruments.

- Study and become familiar with unique geographical conditions where flight is intended.

- Do not attempt visual flight when there is a possibility of being trapped in deteriorating weather.

- If you experience a visual illusion during flight (most pilots do at one time or another), have confidence in your instruments and ignore all conflicting signals your body gives you. Accidents usually happen as a result of a pilot's indecision to rely on the instruments.

- If you are one of two pilots in an aircraft and you begin to experience a visual illusion, transfer control of the aircraft to the other pilot, since pilots seldom experience visual illusions at the same time.

- By being knowledgeable, relying on experience, and trusting your instruments, you will be contributing to keeping the skies safe for everyone.

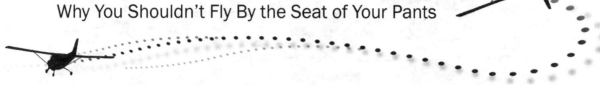

17 | Spatial Disorientation:
Why You Shouldn't Fly By the Seat of Your Pants

Spatial Orientation

Defines our natural ability to maintain our body orientation and/or posture in relation to the surrounding environment (physical space) at rest and during motion. Genetically speaking, humans are designed to maintain spatial orientation on the ground. The three-dimensional environment of flight is unfamiliar to the human body, creating sensory conflicts and illusions that make spatial orientation difficult, and sometimes impossible to achieve. Statistics show that between 5 to 10% of all general aviation accidents can be attributed to spatial disorientation, 90% of which are fatal.

Spatial Orientation in Flight

Spatial orientation in flight is difficult to achieve because numerous sensory stimuli (visual, vestibular, and proprioceptive) vary in magnitude, direction, and frequency. Any differences or discrepancies between visual, vestibular, and proprioceptive sensory inputs result in a sensory mismatch that can produce illusions and lead to spatial disorientation. Good spatial orientation relies on the effective perception, integration and interpretation of visual, vestibular (organs of equilibrium located in the inner ear) and proprioceptive (receptors located in the skin, muscles, tendons, and joints) sensory information.

Vestibular Aspects of Spatial Orientation

The inner ear contains the vestibular system, which is also known as the organ of equilibrium. About the size of an pencil eraser, the vestibular system contains two distinct structures: the semicircular canals, which detect changes in angular acceleration, and the otolith organs (the utricule and the saccule), which detect changes in linear accelera-tion and gravity. Both the semicircular canals and the otolith organs provide information to the brain regarding our body's position and movement. A connection between the vestibular system and the eyes helps to maintain balance and keep the eyes focused on an object while the head is moving or while the body is rotating.

The Semicircular Canals

The semicircular canals are three half-circular, inter-connected tubes located inside each ear that are the equivalent of three gyroscopes located in three planes perpendicular (at right angles) to each other. Each plane corresponds to the rolling, pitching, or yawing motions of an aircraft. [Figure 17.1]

Each canal is filled with a fluid called endolymph and contains a motion sensor with little hairs whose ends are embedded in a gelatinous structure called the cupula. The cupula and the hairs move as the fluid moves inside the canal in response to an an-gular acceleration.

The movement of the hairs is similar to the move-ment of seaweed caused by ocean currents or that of wheat fields moved by wind gusts. When the head is still and the airplane is straight and level, the fluid in the canals does not move and the hairs stand straight up, indicating to the brain that there is no rotational acceleration (a turn).

If you turn either your aircraft or your head, the ca-nal moves with your head, but the fluid inside does not move because of its inertia. As the canal moves, the hairs inside also move with it and are bent in the opposite direction of the acceleration by the stationary fluid [Figure 17.2A]. This hair movement

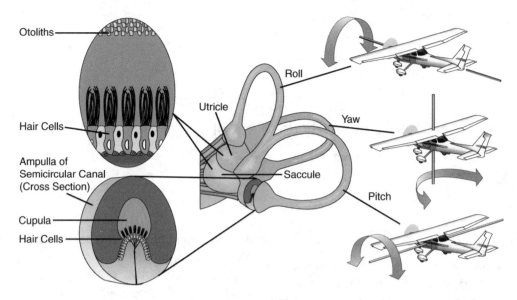

Figure 17.1 The semicircular canals lie in three planes, and sense motions of roll, pitch and yaw.

sends a signal to the brain to indicate that the head has turned. The problem starts when you continue turning your aircraft at a constant rate (as in a coordinated turn) for more than 20 seconds.

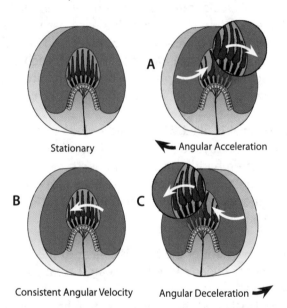

Figure 17.2 The effects of angular acceleration on the semicircular canals.

In this kind of turn, the fluid inside the canal starts moving initially, then friction causes it to catch up with the walls of the rotating canal [Figure 17.2B]. When this happens, the hairs inside the canal will return to their straight up position, sending an erroneous signal to the brain that the turn has stopped—when, in fact, the turn continues.

If you then start rolling out of the turn to go back to level flight, the fluid inside the canal will continue to move (because of its inertia), and the hairs will now move in the opposite direction [Figure 17.2C], sending an erroneous signal to the brain indicating that you are turning in the opposite direction, when in fact, you are actually slowing down from the original turn.

Vestibular Illusions (Somatogyral—Semicircular Canals)

Illusions involving the semicircular canals of the vestibular system occur primarily under conditions of unreliable or unavailable external visual references and result in false sensations of rotation. These include the Leans, the Graveyard Spin and Spiral, and the Coriolis Illusion.

The Leans. This is the most common illusion during flight and is caused by a sudden return to level flight following a gradual and prolonged turn that went unnoticed by the pilot.

The reason a pilot can be unaware of such a gradual turn is that human exposure to a rotational acceleration of 2 degrees per second or lower is below the detection threshold of the semicircular canals. Leveling the wings after such a turn may cause an illusion that the aircraft is banking in the opposite direction. In response to such an illusion, a pilot may lean in the direction of the original turn in a corrective attempt to regain the perception of a correct vertical posture.

The Graveyard Spin is an illusion that can occur to a pilot who intentionally or unintentionally enters a spin. For example, a pilot who enters a spin to the left will initially have a sensation of spinning in the same direction. However, if the left spin continues the pilot will have the sensation that the spin is progressively decreasing. At this point, if the pilot applies right rudder to stop the left spin, the pilot will suddenly sense a spin in the opposite direction (to the right). If the pilot believes that the airplane is spinning to the right, the response will be to apply left rudder to counteract the sensation of a right spin. However, by applying left rudder the pilot will unknowingly re-enter the original left spin. If the pilot cross checks the turn indicator, he/she would see the turn needle indicating a left turn while he/she senses a right turn. This creates a sensory conflict between what the pilot sees on the instruments and what the pilot feels. If the pilot believes the body sensations instead of trusting the instruments, the left spin will continue. If enough altitude is lost before this illusion is recognized and corrective action is taken, impact with terrain is inevitable. [Figure 17.3]

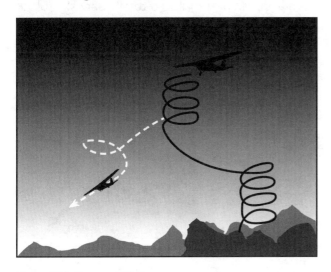

Figure 17.3 Graveyard Spin.

The Graveyard Spiral is more common than the Graveyard Spin, and it is associated with a return to level flight following an intentional or unintentional prolonged bank turn. For example, a pilot who enters a banking turn to the left will initially have a sensation of a turn in the same direction. If the left turn continues (~20 seconds or more), the pilot will experience the sensation that the airplane is no longer turning to the left. At this point, if the pilot attempts to level the wings this action will produce a sensation that the airplane is turning and banking in the opposite direction (to the right). If the pilot believes the illusion of a right turn (which can be very compelling), he/she will re-enter the original left turn in an attempt to counteract the sensation of a right turn. Unfortunately, while this is happening, the airplane is still turning to the left and losing altitude. Pulling the control yoke/stick and applying power while turning would not be a good idea—because it would only make the left turn tighter. If the pilot fails to recognize the illusion and does not level the wings, the airplane will continue turning left and losing altitude until it impacts the ground.

The Coriolis Illusion involves the simultaneous stimulation of two semicircular canals and is associated with a sudden tilting (forward or backwards) of the pilot's head while the aircraft is turning. This can occur when you tilt you head down (to look at an approach chart or to write a note on your knee pad), or tilt it up (to look at an overhead instrument or switch) or tilt it sideways. This produces an almost unbearable sensation that the aircraft is rolling, pitching, and yawing all at the same time, which can be compared with the sensation of rolling down on a hillside. This illusion can make the pilot quickly become disoriented and lose control of the aircraft.

The Otolith Organs

Two otolith organs, the saccule and utricle, are located in each ear and are set at right angles to each other. The utricle detects changes in linear acceleration in the horizontal plane, while the saccule detects gravity changes in the vertical plane. However, the inertial forces resulting from linear accelerations cannot be distinguished from the force of gravity; therefore, gravity can also produce stimulation of the utricle and saccule. These organs are located at the base (vestibule) of the semicircular canals, and their structure consists of small sacs (maculas) covered by hair cell filaments that project into an overlying gelatinous membrane (cupula) tipped by tiny, chalk-like calcium stones called otoconia. [Figure 17.4]

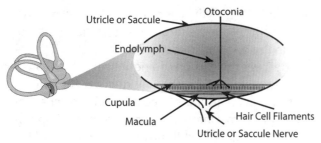

Figure 17.4 Otolith organs.

Change in Gravity

When the head is tilted, the weight of the otoconia of the saccule pulls the cupula, which in turn bends the hairs that send a signal to the brain indicating that the head has changed position. A similar response will occur during a vertical take-off in a helicopter or following the sudden opening of a parachute after a free fall.

Change in Linear Acceleration

The inertial forces resulting from a forward linear acceleration (take-off, increased acceleration during level flight, vertical climb) produce a backward displacement of the otoconia of the utricle that pulls the cupula, which in turn bends the haircell filaments that send a signal to the brain, indicating that the head and body have suddenly been moved forward. Exposure to a backward linear acceleration, or to a forward linear decceleration has the opposite effect. [Figure 17.5]

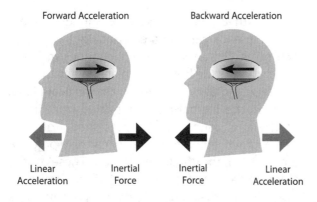

Figure 17.5 Change in linear acceleration.

Vestibular Illusions (Somatogravic — Utricle and Saccule)

Illusions involving the utricle and the saccule of the vestibular system are most likely under conditions with unreliable or unavailable external visual references. These illusions include: the Inversion Illusion, Head-Up Illusion, and Head-Down Illusion.

The **Inversion Illusion** involves a steep ascent (forward linear acceleration) in a high-performance aircraft, followed by a sudden return to level flight. When the pilot levels off, the aircraft's speed is relatively higher. This combination of accelerations produces an illusion that the aircraft is in inverted flight. The pilot's response to this illusion is to lower the nose of the aircraft.

The **Head-Up Illusion** involves a sudden forward linear acceleration during level flight where the pilot perceives the illusion that the nose of the aircraft is pitching up. The pilot's response to this illusion would be to push the yolk or the stick forward to pitch the nose of the aircraft down. A night take-off from a well-lit airport into a totally dark sky (black hole) or a catapult take-off from an aircraft carrier can also lead to this illusion, and could result in a crash. [Figure 17.6]

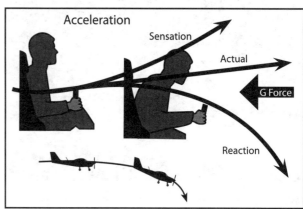

Figure 17.6 Head-up illusion.

The **Head-Down Illusion** involves a sudden linear deceleration (air braking, lowering flaps, decreasing engine power) during level flight where the pilot perceives the illusion that the nose of the aircraft is pitching down. The pilot's response to this illusion would be to pitch the nose of the aircraft up. If this illusion occurs during a low-speed final approach, the pilot could stall the aircraft.

The Proprioceptive Receptors

The proprioceptive receptors (proprioceptors) are special sensors located in the skin, muscles, tendons, and joints that play a very small role in maintaining spatial orientation in normal individuals. Proprioceptors do give some indication of posture by sensing the relative position of our body parts in relation to each other, and by sensing points of physical contact between body parts and the surrounding environment (floor, wall, seat, arm rest, etc.). For example, proprioceptors make it possible for you to know that you are seated while flying; however, they alone will not let you differentiate between flying straight and level and performing a coordinated turn.

How to Prevent Spatial Disorientation

The following are basic steps that should help prevent spatial disorientation:

- Take the opportunity to experience spatial disorientation illusions in a Barany chair, a Vertigon, a GYRO, or a Virtual Reality Spatial Disorientation Demonstrator.

- Before flying with less than 3 miles visibility, obtain training and maintain proficiency in airplane control by reference to instruments.

- When flying at night or in reduced visibility, use the flight instruments.

- If intending to fly at night, maintain night-flight currency. Include cross-country and local operations at different airports.

- If only Visual Flight Rules-qualified, do not attempt visual flight when there is a possibility of getting trapped in deteriorating weather.

- If you experience a vestibular illusion during flight, trust your instruments and disregard your sensory perceptions.

Spatial Disorientation and Airsickness

It is important to know the difference between spatial disorientation and airsickness. Airsickness is a normal response of healthy individuals when exposed to a flight environment characterized by unfamiliar motion and orientation clues. Common signs and symptoms of airsickness include: vertigo, loss of appetite, increased salivation and swallowing, burping, stomach awareness, nausea, retching, vomiting, increased need for bowel movements, cold sweating, skin pallor, sensation of fullness of the head, difficulty concentrating, mental confusion, apathy, drowsiness, difficulty focusing, visual flashbacks, eye strain, blurred vision, increased yawning, headache, dizziness, postural instability, and increased fatigue.

The symptoms are usually progressive. First, the desire for food is lost. Then, as saliva collects in the mouth, the person begins to perspire freely, the head aches, and the airsick person may eventually become nauseated and vomit. Severe airsickness may cause a pilot to become completely incapacitated.

Although airsickness is uncommon among experienced pilots, it does occur occasionally (especially among student pilots). Some people are more susceptible to airsickness than others. Fatigue, alcohol, drugs, medications, stress, illnesses, anxiety, fear, and insecurity are some factors that can increase individual susceptibility to motion sickness of any type. Women have been shown to be more susceptible to motion sickness than men of any age. In addition, reduced mental activity (low mental workload) during exposure to an unfamiliar motion has been implicated as a predisposing factor for airsickness.

A pilot who concentrates on the mental tasks required to fly an aircraft will be less likely to become airsick because his/her attention is occupied. This explains why sometimes a student pilot who is at the controls of an aircraft does not get airsick, but the experienced instructor who is only monitoring the student unexpectedly becomes airsick.

A pilot who has been the victim of airsickness knows how uncomfortable and impairing it can be. Most importantly, it jeopardizes the pilot's flying proficiency and safety, particularly under conditions that require peak piloting skills and performance (equipment malfunctions, instrument flight conditions, bad weather, final approach, and landing).

Pilots who are susceptible to airsickness should not take anti-motion sickness medications (prescription or over-the-counter). These medications can make one drowsy or affect brain functions in other ways. Research has shown that most anti-motion sickness medications cause a temporary deterioration of navigational skills or other tasks demanding keen judgment.

An effective method to increase pilot resistance to airsickness consists of repetitive exposure to the flying conditions that initially resulted in airsickness. In other words, repeated exposure to the flight environment decreases an individual's susceptibility to subsequent airsickness.

If you become airsick while piloting an aircraft, open the air vents, loosen your clothing, use supplemental oxygen, keep your eyes on a point outside the aircraft, place your head against the seat's headrest, and avoid unnecessary head movements. Then, cancel the flight, and land as soon as possible.

FAA Aeromedical Training Programs for Civil Aviation Pilots

Physiological Training Course. The Civil Aerospace Medical Institute offers a 1-day training course to familiarize civil aviation pilots and flight crews with the physiological and psychological stressors of flight. Classroom training subjects include spatial disorientation, oxygen equipment, hypoxia, trapped gas, and decompression sickness.

Demonstrations. Spatial disorientation demonstrators provide pilots the experience of vestibular and visual illusions in a safe, ground-based environment —and they teach ways to avoid spatial disorientation while flying. Also, a ground-based altitude chamber flight offers a practical demonstration of rapid decompression and hypoxia. For information and scheduling, call (405) 954-4837, or check the FAA Web site:
www.faa.gov/pilots/training/airman_education/
aerospace_physiology/index.cfm

18 | Seatbelts and Shoulder Harnesses:
Smart Protection in Small Airplanes

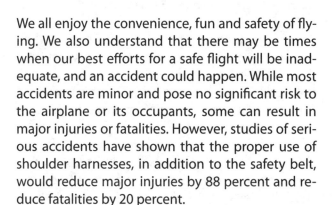

We all enjoy the convenience, fun and safety of flying. We also understand that there may be times when our best efforts for a safe flight will be inadequate, and an accident could happen. While most accidents are minor and pose no significant risk to the airplane or its occupants, some can result in major injuries or fatalities. However, studies of serious accidents have shown that the proper use of shoulder harnesses, in addition to the safety belt, would reduce major injuries by 88 percent and reduce fatalities by 20 percent.

Install Shoulder Harnesses in Your Airplane

Shoulder harnesses have been required for all seats in small airplanes manufactured since December 12, 1986. If your airplane is not equipped with them, you should obtain kits for installing shoulder harnesses from the manufacturer or the manufacturer's local sales representative.

Use the Restraint System Properly

Federal regulations require that safety belts and shoulder harnesses (when installed) be properly worn during landings and takeoffs. If the restraint is not worn properly, it cannot provide full benefits and can even cause injury in a serious impact.

Tests have shown that slack in the restraint system should be minimal. In an impact, your body keeps moving until the slack is taken out of the restraint, but then must be abruptly stopped to "catch up" with the airplane. The restraint should be adjusted as tightly as your comfort will permit to minimize potential injuries. [Figure 18.1]

Figure 18.1 Movement as a result of too much slack in the restraint system.

The safety belt should be placed low on your hip bones so that the belt loads will be taken by the strong skeleton of your body. If the safety belt is improperly positioned on your abdomen, it can cause internal injuries. If the safety belt is positioned on your thighs, rather than the hip bones, it cannot effectively limit your body's forward motion. [Figure 18.2]

Figure 18.2 Proper placement of the safety belt.

Shoulder harness systems can use dual shoulder belts or a single diagonal belt similar to those used in automobiles. The belts should not rub against your head or neck. This is uncomfortable, will discourage use of the shoulder harness, and can also cause neck injuries during an impact. [Figure 18.3]

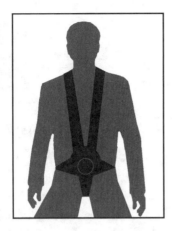

Figure 18.3 *Proper placement of a dual shoulder belt.*

Single diagonal shoulder belts should be positioned so that the torso's center of gravity falls within the angle formed by the shoulder belt and the safety belt. Otherwise your torso may roll right out of the shoulder belt during an impact and compromise your protection. [Figure 18.4]

Figure 18.4 *Proper placement of a single diagonal shoulder belt.*

Because the lower end of the shoulder belt is usually fastened to the safety belt buckle or the buckle insert, the safety belt buckle should be positioned on the side of your hip. This differs from the central location of the buckle that is common when only the safety belt is used. [Figure 18.5]

Figure 18.5 *Correct safety belt buckle location.*

Be sure that the safety belt is installed so that when the buckle is unlatched, both the safety belt and the shoulder belt are released. Also, be sure that the buckle can be unlatched without interference from the seat armrest, aircraft controls, or the interior wall of the airplane.

If the shoulder harness uses dual belts fastened to the safety belt near the center of your body, the shoulder belts will tend to pull the safety belt up off your hip bones. This could cause internal injuries in an impact.

When it is tightened about your hips, the safety belt should be positioned so that it makes an angle of about 55 degrees with the centerline of the airplane. This allows it to resist the upward pull of the shoulder belts, reducing the risk of internal injury. [Figure 18.6]

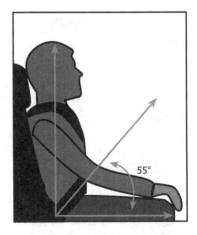

Figure 18.6 *Correct position of safety belt in relation to airplane centerline.*

Otherwise, a tiedown strap from the buckle to the centerforward edge of the seat may be necessary to resist the upward pull of the shoulder belts. [Figure 18.7]

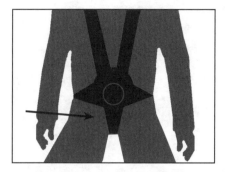

Figure 18.7 Safety belt buckle tiedown strap.

If your restraint system uses a tie-down strap, adjust it to remove all the slack when the restraint system is used. A properly installed and adjusted tie-down strap is completely safe.

Don't Forget the Children

For maximum protection and safety, small children should be placed and secured in approved "child safety seat" devices during aircraft operation. Child safety seats must meet current manufacturing and identification requirements of the Federal government and be installed and secured in accordance with these regulations. Install the safety seat in a rear airplane seat, but not near an entry door or emergency exit. If you must use a front airplane seat, make sure that the child seat cannot interfere with the airplane controls or limit pilot access to the radios and flight instruments. Install the child safety seat according to the instructions on the seat, using the airplane safety belt to secure it. Most safety seats for small infants are intended to place the infant in a rear-facing position and should be installed that way in the airplane. [Figure 18.8]

Remember to consider the weight of the child and child safety seat when calculating weight and balance!

Figure 18.8 Child safety seat.

When children outgrow the safety seat, they can safely get by using only the airplane seat belt. Their small size limits the chance that they might make contact with the airplane interior during an impact. Larger children can use the shoulder harness if it doesn't rub on their face or neck when they are seated.

Summary

- Seatbelts alone will protect you only in minor impacts.
- Using shoulder belts in small aircraft would reduce major injuries by 88% and fatalities by 20%.
- Shoulder belt kits are now available for most airplanes.
- Proper use and installation of child safety seats, meeting Federal requirements, provide good protection for small children in aircraft.
- If improperly installed and used, restraints could cause injury.
- Restraint systems in small aircraft: a smart idea!

19 | Flying with Passengers

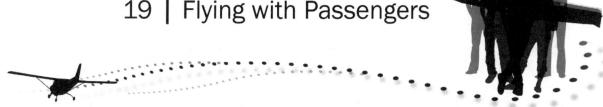

Passengers come in all sizes, shapes, and temperaments. It is not uncommon for a pilot to take up a friend who is ordinarily calm and relaxed, only to find that he becomes completely unnerved and panicky during some incidental flight mishap.

All of us operate at two levels: the rational and the emotional. Our daily activities are regulated by the rational forces—logic, knowledge, experience, and goal-seeking. But under this exterior, strong emotions lie dormant—fear, anger, and love, for example. Fear, or more accurately, anxiety, is the emotion most often encountered in flying. Many passengers have some vague, weakly formulated anxiety about "what might happen up there." Then, if some minor mishap occurs, they experience a natural "fight-or-flight" response (the instinctive reaction of a human being to danger).

Obviously, though, they have no suitable object at hand to fight, and flight (in the sense of escape) is out of the question. So the anxious passenger tries to appear calm while enduring inner torment and tension. His nervousness may be apparent in chain-smoking, heavy perspiring, rambling conversation, stony silence, or other peculiar behavior. Strangely enough, his very effort to conceal his fear and combat his growing tension just leads to greater anxiety.

If you are carrying several passengers, one of them can quickly infect the others with his anxiety. And a group of panicky passengers can be a threat to safe flight. Bear in mind that others may not be as confident in the air as you, and take precautions to minimize their discomfort and worry. Keep flight maneuvers smooth and professional. Avoid sudden control movements, uncertainty in selecting your course or destination, requests for radio assistance, or any behavior which might undermine your passengers' faith in your skill and self-confidence.

All the medical problems discussed previously in this handbook apply to passengers as well as to pilots. The remedial steps suggested for you as the pilot should be the same for your passengers, and should be taken before any difficulty magnifies itself. However, a few medical situations apply solely to passengers.

Before allowing a pregnant woman to fly in your aircraft (especially if she has a history of miscarriages), have her check with her physician. The decreased pressure at altitude may be inadvisable. If a passenger has brought an infant along, the baby should either be made to cry or given a bottle or pacifier during descent to keep the Eustachian tubes open.

If a passenger shows signs of airsickness during flight, encourage him to look out the window at a fixed, definite object; the horizon, faraway clouds, or a distant object on the ground is suitable. The commonly available motion sickness medications are also useful for relieving the discomfort. Persons who are bothered with nasal congestion associated with altitude may obtain effective remedies from their physician or pharmacist.

If you are transporting a sick person, keep in mind the effects of altitude on his particular condition. Those with a history of cardiovascular or pulmonary problems should be very closely observed. Bowel obstructions may become aggravated by the expansion of trapped gas. Some types of hernia may worsen for the same reason.

Your own confidence and control of the aircraft, along with an awareness of your passengers' needs, will help ensure a relaxed and safe flight for everyone.

20 | Medical Certification: Questions & Answers

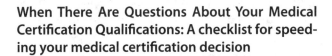

When There Are Questions About Your Medical Certification Qualifications: A checklist for speeding your medical certification decision

Most (more than 90%) medical certification applicants pass their physical examinations, and the Aviation Medical Examiner (AME) is able to issue a medical certificate at the time of the exam. Occasionally, however, a condition is found that requires a process of further review and, possibly, additional testing. The purpose of this brochure is to help answer some of the questions that you might have about this process.

What are my chances of ultimately being certified?

While it is impossible to predict your individual likelihood of certification, our current process allows us ultimately to certify 96% of individuals whose medical qualifications are initially questioned. Sometimes this process requires a period of recovery from an illness, surgery, or other condition.

Why does it take so long to process my application and other reports?

We receive an average of 1,800 applications for medical certification each day. We are required to review each to assure that medical standards are met. When an application is found that may not meet the requirements, a letter is written to the applicant identifying the problem and outlining the further potential courses of action. We must then wait for a response from the applicant before we can proceed further. Each time new information is received, the application package must again be reviewed. Given the large number of applications being processed and the amount of time required

to evaluate the information, it sometimes takes longer than we would like.

What can I do to speed the process along?

There are several steps you can take to assure that your application package is processed in the shortest time possible. Use this list of items like a checklist to speed the processing of your application.

- Don't hesitate to ask your AME for advice and assistance in gathering the requested information.

- When we ask for additional information, we ask for the least amount possible to make our decision. This means that we really do need everything that we request, so the first thing that you can do is to make sure that all the information that we have requested is being provided. Also, please understand, if we ask that a certain test be performed in a certain way, that is what we need. Be sure that you take all of our letters with you to your physician, and try to emphasize the importance of exactly fulfilling our requests.

- Have all of the requested information forwarded to us in one package.

- Do not hide important medical facts from us. This just delays things further. If you send us information about one medical problem and the hospital records indicate a second serious medical problem, which we did not previously know about, we will have to start a new investigation of the second problem.

- Give us an adequate amount of time to process your application. If you call or write to find out the status of your application, your file will have to be located and taken out of line to answer the inquiry. This will further delay its processing. On the other hand, if you haven't heard from us within 60 days, you may call us at the number listed below for an update.

If my own physician thinks I'm okay to fly, why do you have a problem with me?

Most physicians see their role as one of helping their patients by preventing medical problems when possible and treating medical problems if they do occur. This treatment may actually be a cure or it may be something that diminishes the impact of the medical condition on the person's daily life.

There are many conditions that can be cured, such as appendicitis, gall bladder disease, and pneumonia. There are other conditions that can be treated but are not cured, such as high blood pressure, heart disease, and diabetes.

In the case of this latter group, when a physician has done all that is possible to control the disease, the patient may be told that participation in any ac-

tivity, including flying, is okay. To the treating physician, this means that there is nothing more to be done for the disease, and that activity will not make the disease worse.

Unfortunately, the treating physician does not always realize that the medical condition could make the activity worse (by making it less safe due to the medical condition). In addition, many physicians only fly as passengers on commercial aircraft. They do not realize the potential problems inherent in piloting aircraft, which may require more from the pilot than his or her medical condition will allow.

Medical Certification Checklist

❏ Ask AME to help
❏ Send all data to FAA
❏ Send all in one packet
❏ Don't hide facts
❏ Allow enough time for FAA to process file

Glossary

Active noise reduction headsets. A headset that uses active noise reduction technology that allows the manipulation of sound and signal waves to reduce noise, improve signal-to-noise ratios, and enhance sound quality.

Aerial Perspective Illusions. Caused by runways with different widths, upsloping or downsloping runways, and upsloping or downsloping final approach terrain. These illusions may make you change (increase or decrease) the slope of your final approach.

Aeronautical decision making (ADM). A systematic approach to the mental process used by airplane pilots to consistently determine the best course of action in response to a given set of circumstances.

Airsickness. A normal response of healthy individuals when exposed to a flight environment characterized by unfamiliar motion and orientation clues.

Altitude-induced decompression sickness. Decompression sickness occurring during exposure to altitude.

Astigmatism. A condition often caused from an irregular curvature of the cornea. As a result, light is not focused to a single image on the retina.

Attitude management. The ability to recognize hazardous attitudes in oneself and the willingness to modify them as necessary through the application of an appropriate antidote thought.

Attitude. A personal motivational predisposition to respond to persons, situations, or events in a given manner that can, nevertheless, be changed or modified through training as sort of a mental shortcut to decision making.

Autokinetic illusion. Gives the impression that a stationary object is moving in front of the airplane's path. It is caused by staring at a fixed single point of light (ground light or a star) in a totally dark and featureless background.

Aviation Medical Examiner (AME). A physician with training in aviation medicine designated by the Civil Aerospace Medical Institute (CAMI). They can accept applications for physical examinations necessary for issuing medical certificates.

Black-hole approach illusion. Can happen during a final approach at night (no stars or moonlight) over water or unlighted terrain to a lighted runway beyond which the horizon is not visible.

Blind spot. The area where the optic nerve connects to the retina in the back of each eye is known as the optic disk. There is a total absence of cones and rods in this area, and, consequently, each eye is completely blind in this spot.

Carbon monoxide. A colorless and odorless gas that is a by-product of the incomplete combustion of carbon-containing materials such as aviation fuel.

Carbon monoxide poisoning. Oxygen starvation to the brain caused when carbon monoxide is inhaled. Carbon monoxide leaks can occur with faulty heating systems in aircraft or when there is cigarette smoking in the cockpit.

Central vision. Involved with the identification of objects and the perception of colors. Also known as foveal vision.

Cones. Located in higher concentrations than rods in the central area of the retina known as the macula. The cones are used for day or high-intensity light vision. They are involved with central vision to detect detail, perceive color, and identify far-away objects.

Coriolis illusion. An abrupt head movement in a prolonged constant-rate turn that has ceased stimulating the motion sensing system can create the illusion of rotation or movement in an entirely different axis. The disoriented pilot will maneuver the aircraft into a dangerous attitude in an attempt to stop rotation. This most overwhelming of all illusions in flight may be prevented by not making sudden, extreme head movements, particularly while making prolonged constant-rate turns under IFR conditions.

Crew resource management (CRM). The application of team management concepts in the flight deck environment. It was initially known as cockpit resource management, but as CRM programs evolved to include cabin crews, maintenance personnel, and others, the phrase crew resource management was adopted. This includes single pilots, as in most general aviation aircraft. Pilots of small aircraft, as well as crews of larger aircraft, must make effective use of all available resources; human resources, hardware, and information. A current definition includes all groups routinely working with the cockpit crew who are involved in decisions required to operate a flight safely. These groups include, but are not limited to: pilots, dispatchers, cabin crewmembers, maintenance personnel, and air traffic controllers. CRM is one way of addressing the challenge of optimizing the human/machine interface and accompanying interpersonal activities.

Dark adaptation. The process by which the eyes adapt for optimal night visual acuity under conditions of low ambient illumination.

Decide model. A six-step model developed using the acronym "DECIDE" to assist in remembering the elements of the decision-making process.

Decision-making process. Steps involving the examination changes that have occurred, the gathering information, and assessment risk before reaching a decision and choosing a course of action.

Decompression sickness (DCS). A condition characterized by a variety of symptoms resulting from exposure to low barometric pressures that cause inert gases (mainly nitrogen), normally dissolved in body fluids and tissues, to come out of physical solution and form bubbles.

Duration. Determines the quality of the perception and discrimination of a sound, as well as the potential risk of hearing impairment when exposed to high intensity sounds.

Ear block. A situation where congestion around the Eustachian tubes in the ear make equalization difficult when descending to lower altitudes in flight. Consequently, the difference in pressure between the middle ear and aircraft cabin can build up to a level that will hold the Eustachian tube closed, making equalization difficult if not impossible.

External resources. Resources found outside of the cockpit during flight. These include air traffic controllers and flight service specialists.

False visual reference illusions. Caused by flying over a banked cloud, night flying over featureless terrain with ground lights that are indistinguishable from a dark sky with stars, or night flying over a featureless terrain with a clearly defined pattern of ground lights and a dark, starless sky.

Fatigue. A condition characterized by increased discomfort with lessened capacity for work, reduced efficiency of accomplishment, loss of power or capacity to respond to stimulation, and is usually accompanied by a feeling of weariness and tiredness.

Fire. A complex, dynamic, physicochemical event and is the result of a rapid chemical reaction generating smoke, heat, flame, and light.

Fovea. The small depression located in the exact center of the macula that contains a high concentration of cones but no rods, and this is where our vision is most sharp.

Frequency. The physical property of sound that gives it a pitch.

Graveyard spin. A proper recovery from a spin that has ceased stimulating the motion sensing system can create the illusion of spinning in the opposite direction. The disoriented pilot will return the aircraft to its original spin.

Graveyard spiral. An observed loss of altitude during a coordinated constant-rate turn that has ceased stimulating the motion sensing system can create the illusion of being in a descent with the wings level. The disoriented pilot will pull back on the controls, tightening the spiral and increasing the loss of altitude.

Hazardous attitudes. Attitudes that can interfere with the ability to make sound decisions and exercise authority properly.

Head-down illusion. Involves a sudden linear deceleration (air braking, lowering flaps, decreasing engine power) during level flight where the pilot perceives the illusion that the nose of the aircraft is pitching down. The pilot's response to this illusion would be to pitch the nose of the aircraft up. If this illusion occurs during a low-speed final approach, the pilot could stall the aircraft.

Head-up illusion. Involves a sudden forward linear acceleration during level flight where the pilot perceives the illusion that the nose of the aircraft is pitching up. The pilot's response to this illusion would be to push the yolk or the stick forward to pitch the nose of the aircraft down. A night take-off from a well-lit airport into a totally dark sky (black hole) or a catapult take-off from an aircraft carrier can also lead to this illusion, and could result in a crash.

Headwork. Required to accomplish a conscious, rational thought process when making decisions. Good decision making involves risk identification and assessment, information processing, and problem solving.

Hearing. The process, function, or power of perceiving sound.

Human factors. The study of how people interact with their environments. In the case of general aviation, it is the study of how pilot performance is influenced by such issues as the design of cockpits, the function of the organs of the body, the effects of emotions, and the interaction and communication with the other participants of the aviation community, such as other crewmembers and air traffic control personnel.

Hyperbaric oxygen treatment. 100% oxygen delivered in a high-pressure chamber.

Hyperopia. A condition in which light rays are focused behind the retina. An estimated 40% of Americans are hyperopic. Also referred to as farsightedness, where near objects appear fuzzy.

Hyperventilation. An abnormal increase in the volume of air breathed in and out of the lungs.

Hypoxia. A condition in which the brain is starved of oxygen. Pilots are susceptible to hypoxia during flights at high altitude where no supplemental oxygen is used.

I'M SAFE checklist. A checklist for pilots to evaluate their fitness for flight.

IFR. Instrument Flight Rules. For the purpose of this book, it is defined as a ceiling less than 1,000 feet AGL and/or visibility less than three miles.

Intensity. The correlation between sound intensity and loudness.

Internal resources. Resources found in the cockpit during flight. These include the ingenuity, knowledge, and skill of the pilot, advanced navigation and autopilot systems, checklists, the Airplane Flight Manual/Pilot's Operating Handbook (AFM/POH), current aeronautical charts, Airport/Facility Directory, and passengers.

Inversion illusion. Involves a steep ascent (forward linear acceleration) in a high-performance aircraft, followed by a sudden return to level flight. When the pilot levels off, the aircraft's speed is relatively higher. This combination of accelerations produces an illusion that the aircraft is in inverted flight. The pilot's response to this illusion is to lower the nose of the aircraft.

Iris. The colored part of the eye that controls the opening (dilation) and closing (constriction) of the pupil.

Judgment. The mental process of recognizing and analyzing all pertinent information in a particular situation, a rational evaluation of alternative actions in response to it, and a timely decision on which action to take.

LASIK. Laser in situ Keratomileusis procedure by the use of one of these devices: the microkeratome and excimer laser. During the LASIK procedure, the microkeratome slices a thin flap from the top of the cornea, leaving it connected by a small hinge of tissue. The corneal flap is folded aside and the excimer laser is used to reshape the underlying corneal stroma. The flap is then returned to its original position.

Lens. Located behind the pupil and its function is to focus light on the surface of the retina.

Medical certificate. Acceptable evidence of physical fitness on a form prescribed by the Administrator.

Mesopic vision. Occurs at dawn, dusk, or under full moonlight levels, and is characterized by decreasing visual acuity and color vision. Under these conditions, a combination of central (foveal cones) and peripheral (rods) vision is required to maintain appropriate visual performance.

Monocular vision. Having only one eye or effective visual acuity equivalent to monocular (i.e. best corrected distant visual acuity in the poorer eye is no better than 20/200).

Myopia. A condition in which light rays are focused in front of the retina. About 30% of Americans are myopic. Also referred to as nearsightedness, where distant objects appear fuzzy.

Night blind spot. Appears under conditions of low ambient illumination due to the absence of rods in the fovea, and involves an area 5 to 10 degrees wide in the center of the visual field. Therefore, if an object is viewed directly at night, it may go undetected or it may fade away after initial detection due to the night blind spot.

Noise. A sound, especially one which lacks agreeable musical quality, is noticeably unpleasant, or is too loud.

Operational pitfalls. Behavioral traps into which pilots have been known to fall. Trying to complete a flight as planned, please passengers, and meet schedules can have an adverse effect on safety, and can impose an unrealistic assessment of piloting skills under stressful conditions. These tendencies ultimately may bring about practices that are dangerous and often illegal, and may lead to a mishap.

Optic disk. The area where the optic nerve connects to the retina in the back of each eye.

Optic nerve. Transmits the pattern of light that strikes the cones and rods as electrical impulses to the brain where these signals are interpreted as an image.

Otolith organs. The saccule and utricle are located in each ear and are set at right angles to each other. The utricle detects changes in linear acceleration in the horizontal plane, while the saccule detects gravity changes in the vertical plane. These organs are located at the base (vestibule) of the semicircular canals, and their structure consists of small sacs (maculas) covered by hair cell filaments that project into an overlying gelatinous membrane (cupula) tipped by tiny, chalk-like calcium stones called otoconia.

Peripheral vision. Involved with the perception of movement (self and surrounding environment) and provides peripheral reference cues to maintain spatial orientation. Also known as ambient vision.

Personal minimums. An individual pilot's set of procedures, rules, criteria, and guidelines for deciding whether, and under what conditions, to operate (or continue operating) in the National Airspace System.

Personality. The embodiment of personal traits and characteristics of an individual that are set at a very early age and extremely resistant to change.

Photopic vision. During daytime or high intensity artificial illumination conditions, the eyes rely on central vision (foveal cones) to perceive and interpret sharp images and color of objects.

Photorefractive Keratectomy (PRK). A procedure that improves visual acuity by altering the curvature of the cornea through a series of laser pulses. PRK can be used to correct myopia, hyperopia, and astigmatism.

Physical stress. Conditions associated with the environment, such as temperature and humidity extremes, noise, vibration, and lack of oxygen.

Physiological stress. Physical conditions, such as fatigue, lack of physical fitness, sleep loss, missed meals (leading to low blood sugar levels), and illness.

Pilot error. An action or decision made by the pilot was the cause, or a contributing factor that led to an accident. This also includes the pilot's failure to make a decision or take action.

Pneumothorax. Trapped gasses in the lungs cause the lungs to collapse.

Poor judgment chain. A series of mistakes that may lead to an accident or incident. Two basic principles generally associated with the creation of a poor judgment chain are: (1) One bad decision often leads to another; and (2) as a string of bad decisions grows, it reduces the number of subsequent alternatives for continued safe flight. ADM is intended to break the poor judgment chain before it can cause an accident or incident. Also referred to as the error chain.

Proprioceptive. Receptors located in the skin, muscles, tendons, and joints.

Psychological stress. Social or emotional factors, such as a death in the family, a divorce, a sick child, or a demotion at work. This type of stress may also be related to mental workload, such as analyzing a problem, navigating an aircraft, or making decisions.

Pupil. Controls the amount of light entering the eye.

Refractive error. Prevents light rays from being brought to a single focus on the retina resulting in reduced visual acuity.

Retina. The inner layer of the eyeball that contains photosensitive cells called rods and cones. The function of the retina is similar to that of the film in a photographic camera: to record an image.

Risk elements in ADM. Take into consideration the four fundamental risk elements: the pilot, the aircraft, the environment, and the type of operation that comprise any given aviation situation.

Risk management. The part of the decision making process which relies on situational awareness, problem recognition, and good judgment to reduce risks associated with each flight.

Rods. Located mainly in the periphery of the retina—an area that is about 10,000 times more sensitive to light than the fovea. Rods are used for low-light intensity or night vision and are involved with peripheral vision to detect position references including objects (fixed and moving) in shades of grey, but cannot be used to detect detail or to perceive color.

Scotopic vision. During nighttime, partial moonlight, or low intensity artificial illumination conditions, central vision (foveal cones) becomes ineffective to maintain visual acuity and color perception. Under these conditions, if you look directly at an object for more than a few seconds, the image of the object fades away completely (night blind spot).

Semicircular canals. Three half-circular, interconnected tubes located inside each ear. Each canal is filled with a fluid called endolymph and contains a motion sensor with little hairs whose ends are embedded in a gelatinous structure called the cupula. The cupula and the hairs move as the fluid moves inside the canal in response to an angular acceleration.

Sinus block. A situation in which congestion around a sinus opening slows pressure equalization of the sinuses that eventually may lead to the opening becoming plugged.

Situational awareness. The accurate perception and understanding of all the factors and conditions within the four fundamental risk elements that affect safety before, during, and after the flight.

Skills and procedures. The procedural, psychomotor, and perceptual skills used to control a specific aircraft or its systems. They are the airmanship abilities that are gained through conventional training, are perfected, and become almost automatic through experience.

Smoke. A complex of particulate matter, as well as a variety of invisible combustion gases and vapors suspended in the fire atmosphere.

Sound. The mechanical radiant energy that is transmitted by longitudinal pressure waves in a medium (solid, liquid, or gas).

Spatial orientation. Our natural ability to maintain our body orientation and/or posture in relation to the surrounding environment (physical space) at rest and during motion.

Stress management. The personal analysis of the kinds of stress experienced while flying, the application of appropriate stress assessment tools, and other coping mechanisms.

Supplemental oxygen. Aviation oxygen should be used during flights at high altitude to combat hypoxia. Regulations state: a 30-minute limit before oxygen is required on flights between 12,500 and 14,000 feet MSL, and immediately upon exposure to cabin pressures above 14,000 feet MSL. For best protection, you are encouraged to use supplemental oxygen above 10,000 feet MSL.

The bends. Joint pain caused when nitrogen dissolved in the body comes out of solution too rapidly either from flying at high altitudes in unpressurized aircraft or during a rapid decompression.

The leans. This is the most common illusion during flight and is caused by a sudden return to level flight following a gradual and prolonged turn that went unnoticed by the pilot. Leveling the wings after such a turn may cause an illusion that the aircraft is banking in the opposite direction.

Vection illusion. An illusion that you are moving opposite to objects around you. A common example is when you are stopped at a traffic light in your car and the car next to you edges forward. Your brain interprets this peripheral visual information as though you are moving backwards and makes you apply additional pressure to the brakes. A similar illusion can happen while taxiing an aircraft.

Vestibular. Organs of equilibrium located in the inner ear.

VFR. Visual Flight Rules. For the purpose of this book, it is defined as a ceiling greater than 3,000 feet AGL and visibility greater than five miles.

Workload management. Ensuring that essential operations are accomplished by planning, prioritizing, and sequencing tasks to avoid work overload.

Bibliography

Many of the government publications used in this compilation are available online and are noted with a web address below whenever this is the case. Some of the material used is now out of circulation.

Section 1   **Aeronautical Decision Making and Risk Management**
Excerpted from Pilot's Handbook of Aeronautical Knowledge, FAA 8083-25, Chapter 17

Section 2   **Establishing Personal Minimums**
Federal Aviation Administration Pilot Safety Brochures,
https://www.faasafety.gov/files/gslac/library/documents/2006/Oct/9091/Developing%20
Personal%20Minimums.pdf

Section 3   **Medications and Flying**
Federal Aviation Administration Pilot Safety Brochures,
http://www.faa.gov/pilots/safety/pilotsafetybrochures/media/Meds_flying_web.pdf

Section 4   **Alcohol and Flying: A Deadly Combination**
Federal Aviation Administration Pilot Safety Brochures,
http://www.faa.gov/pilots/safety/pilotsafetybrochures/media/alcohol.pdf

Section 5   **Fatigue in Aviation**
Federal Aviation Administration Pilot Safety Brochures,
http://www.faa.gov/pilots/safety/pilotsafetybrochures/media/Fatigue_Aviation.pdf

Section 6   **Fitness for Flight**
Excerpted from Aeronautical Information Manual, Chapter 8 Medical Facts for Pilots, Section 1 Fitness for Flight.

Section 7   **Trapped Gas**
http://www.faa.gov/other_visit/aviation_industry/designees_delegations/designee_types/
ame/tutorial/section2/ap_environmental/

Section 8   **Hearing and Noise in Aviation**
Federal Aviation Administration Pilot Safety Brochures,
http://www.faa.gov/pilots/safety/pilotsafetybrochures/media/hearing_brochure.pdf

Section 9   **Altitude-Induced Decompression Sickness**
Federal Aviation Administration Pilot Safety Brochures,
http://www.faa.gov/pilots/safety/pilotsafetybrochures/media/DCS.pdf